Two Essays

(2021)

*

1. A Critique of the Spirit of Criticism (also called the modern spirit or the Antichrist)

*

2. Nature and Human Nature

*

Traumear

Paperback ISBN 978-1-008-98305-2

*

www.traumear.com

*

First essay: The spirit that keeps us in bondage at a time when the preconditions for our freedom exist, (which time is now) may be recognized and banished on three different fronts if we keep our wits about us and familiarize ourselves with who we are, with why we believe we are around and with what we do and why we do it.

Second essay: It may surprise us when we learn what a difference we make between our own human nature and the nature that populates our environment. The sameness, similarities and differences of the two are accentuated in this essay.

*

Critique of the Spirit of Criticism
(also called the modern spirit or the Antichrist)

If we consider, for a moment, what we do when we disagree with someone, it may well occur to us that we quite usually leave our own opinion behind and concentrate entirely on what has annoyed us. In other words, we alter our point of view for the purpose of making a more just appraisal of something or perhaps simply for trying another point of view on for size while we explain why we disagree with it.

Then we might stand back and ask ourselves where we get our knowledge from, our various reflections and insights. Were we born with them? Did we gather them up during a lifetime of surviving by the skin of our teeth or while living high on the hog with not a care in the world? We are quite sure of ourselves, as we can tell by the tone of our voice, how loud it is and evidently persuasive because no one contradicts us.

These are all like little victories, are they not, over those who dare to compare themselves to us as though we shared with them some common denominator – which, by the way, we would strenuously deny, if challenged. Our individuality is our identity. We have based our existence on it and if it crumbles we go down with it. Lord knows, everybody is the same. If we didn't fight our corner we would be gobbled up.

So everyone is the same in that everyone is perfectly different. It boils down to that. It's not meant to make sense. Sense, good or bad, is not the issue here. We want to be known, preferably as someone, and hopefully as someone to be reckoned with. Then we can show our face in public and say: Here I stand, I dare you to stand up to me.

Or we know we are clever and we hide in the hole of some public inconvenience. That would be the other side of the coin. If they knew what they're missing! Quietly we continue, throughout the day, to play our role. In part, this role was foisted upon us and we were too weak and cowardly to shrug it off, however mostly we invented it ourselves, by means of our daily, clever avoidances of revealing to any living soul who we are and what we really mean. We keep our peace and cling to our sense of being well enough informed. We are perfectly ready, at the drop of the hat, to agree with anyone on any topic. The separation between what we really mean and what we are willing to swear to is complete. We feel equally at home on either side of that primordial, plastic lie – we were evidently born with it and we shall remain true to it.

*

So it seems we have the choice to strut or to duck. These are two different goals. The one is achieved, by means of ego-worship and the other is maintained, by keeping our private and our public self as discrete as possible.

Now a human being comes along and, upon due reflection, says: I'm sorry, but I cannot see myself in either one of these – whatever you want to call them. If I were to 'strut', as you call it, something, or someone, would trip me up and if I were to 'duck', in other words if I were to think of my existence as necessarily either private or public, I would sicken or I would be shamed. So yes, I recognize the strutting and the ducking as distinct possibilities but I would never entertain them as goals. Indeed, if I were to sicken or to be shamed, I might say: Aha, I must have made the mistake of attempting to be private or public and if something were to trouble me I would consider that I probably brought it on myself egotistically. However in neither case will I think much about it because I will be too busy reinstating myself in my human being.

And does that really mean something? we feel inclined to ask, this reinstating oneself in one's human being?

Well, yes it does. Where would we be without our human being? Well, we actually know where we would be. We would be sick and shamed or arrogant. And what's more, we would be trying to make a virtue out of it. We would know and see only others like ourselves and so we would not hesitate to insist, if prompted, that we are human beings. However we would be wrong. Due to the fact that we would not be able to recognize human beings we would only rarely be persuaded to question our sense of self. Of course if we ever did question it, there would be hope for us.

* *

As human beings – even as fully fledged human beings – we are, from time to time, tempted.

However what does this mean, to be tempted, once we have thoroughly made ourselves at home in human being? Does it mean that we are being persuaded, by hook or by crook, to be bad or evil? to commit an offence against truth or beauty? To fall away from our high standards?

No, none of these. We are merely being asked to consider, for a moment, the possibility of being less than human. And what is more, there is no way of getting around these periodic temptations. Why is that? Because as human beings we grow. And if I said that as human beings we live, I would not be saying anything substantially different.

Humanity is the essence of being and the substance of human being and if we find ourselves tempted, what this means is that our humanity is saying: Please pay attention to me or else.

So quite possibly, if we have never seriously thought about it, we may have to redefine what we mean by temptation. Since growth takes time and since life involves eternal time, temptation might be described as ‘time on the loose’; time crying out: I don’t want to be left on the shelf!

Indeed, for human beings, timelessness is a threat; or at least something to which we need to pay attention. Without time we are mere time-servers without knowing it. And temptation, if it is to make any sense at all, is a feeling, an apprehension, in fact an apprehensive feeling – which we welcome like good advice from a friend. It’s a bit like the feeling that if we don't start pedalling we will fall over. I cannot imagine any reason why we should not be perfectly familiar with it – and grateful for it.

Unless, of course, we have begun, to any degree at all, to strut or to duck. It would mean that we have ignored temptation for quite a while and it is beginning to insist on itself, thankfully. We evidently need a more appropriate reminder.

So now temptation looks different to us. Now it presents as a downright threat. Pull yourself together mate, or you're in trouble. Practice self-discipline or you'll be sorry.

Quite possibly we won't take the hint. We're too far gone. So we insist on strutting. (You can't tell me what to do!) Or we duck even more and we say: I am the victim. Soothe me. I am the patient. Tend to me. In short, we behave badly. Later on, if by choice or good fortune we have returned to our old self, we might say: I was tempted to behave badly. I fell into temptation.

How inappropriate is that! You were tempted to catch yourself on but you cried: Temptation, go away! It's high time you understood what it really means to be tempted – that is to say, if you wish to join the community of human beings.

*

Now we have to ask: where, in all this, does the critical spirit come into its own? Certainly it does not tempt us. We have shown that we are tempted by time itself, if we pay insufficient attention, to it and to our growth. Neither does it threaten us nor does it try to frighten us into a volte face, away from our human being. No, what it does is, it simply supplies us with an alternative to human being. If you should find, it says, that human being is too much trouble or, let's face it, that it's a bit of a trumped up affair to begin with, then here am I, critical spirit, at your service. You will find that I supply an energy that is quite exemplary. I mean that it shows itself as 'ready for anything', if you know what I mean. Ready for anything and anyone. Energy – a most peculiar energy, to be sure –

is really what I mean by my primary contribution to what I call life. If you want to live, be energetic. In fact, I usually add the spice of: be more energetic than the next fellow, do you know what I mean? I do delight in setting up these agonic competitions all over the place, the meaning of which is not a delightful exercise of gamesmanship, which I find rather uninteresting, but rather, if you'll pardon the expression, a demonstration of 'dog-eat-dog'. Top dog gets the bone? No, sorry, that would be a misunderstanding of what I mean. The essence of the competitive exercise is always simply to kill the opponent. You all have that in you, inside you, don't you know, that desire to kill somebody. To murder the one next to you. Before he murders you? No, that's a miss again. I don't get involved in survival. Survival is something I look down on with a mixture of irony, pity and downright contempt. The idea, my idea, the idea that I am – is to destroy all that stands in the way of self-expression and self-realization. First I would persuade you to isolate your self and get to know it, because that is what you need in order to flesh out your identity – which is no mean thing. You know how much we all like to do for what these days is called Society; (it had different names during the past two millennia). And what do we need, if Society, this marvellous supernatural myth, is to thrive? We need a sufficient number of self-confessed selfs and identities. Oh yes, it's as simple as that. The more you concentrate on that sort of thing, the less you will be bothered with this business of human being, which, let's face it, no one really takes seriously. In any case, in the end it's all about how you apply your labels. If you call a demon a human or even a genius often enough, the label will stick. Now there seem to be a few who are actually born human, so I would ask you simply to ignore those, before they cause you problems. As for those who go out of their way to become human beings, well, we cannot stop them but we can demonstrate to them how successful we are – if we are successful, and there is no reason I can see why we should not be successful. Actually, especially over the past few centuries, the rate at which we have produced sheer marvels of success has risen exponentially. So enjoy these to your heart's content and depend on them to last forever, because that will give you a reason for continuing to exist in this crisis which I am trying to make as normal and supportable as possible.

*

When the critical spirit speaks of a crisis, what does it mean? Here we have something we can get our teeth into. Certainly, as human beings, what we mean by a crisis will not be just precisely the same as what the critical spirit means by it, that goes without saying, surely. What we mean by a crisis is a growth-crisis. We understand crisis in terms of growth. Critical spirit is not interested in growth but in status quo and system-building. So once again we have to make up our mind here. Do we want to be human beings or not. If yes, then a crisis is something we want to 'weather through'. It's as if elementary nature were wanting to be involved in our human being and we ask ourselves: Oh dear, how did that happen? How could we have forgotten about the elements?

What are the elements? They are the very basis of true reality. We incorporate the elements while we grow. Elementary nature is part and parcel of our resurrectional development and evolution – especially of our evolution. We discover it in ourselves while we search for our own meaning within ourselves. We begin by taking an interest in our human nature. We look for it outside ourselves and fail. Then we look within and things begin to make sense. We discover that we are. That we have being. Human being, in particular. And our nature is what we mean, then, when we realize that we grow. That we advance in meaning and in power. As natural beings, meanwhile, we look around and see a multitude of other natural beings, animals, plants, etc. which, like ourselves, participate in birth and death.

When we are done looking around, we look within ourselves and come upon the truth. Most unusual. The truth greets us as a person that lived two millennia ago and lives again within us. What it means – and truth always means something – is that we human beings are all joined, like branches, to one central stem upon which our very life-blood depends. We relate in terms not of trumped up status quo and system but in terms of this particular human being. And the value that is announced by this being is merciful good spirit which fathers us.

"Tripe!" cries critical spirit. "Why can they not leave this Jesus character out of the picture? Always and again they bring him up, now like this, now like that, as if we could not get along just fine without him. Look at these marvellous systems we are developing that are promising to create a status quo for us beyond all previous status quos in sheer magnificence!"

Ah, but you see, the Jesus-character is not what we mean. It is the meaning itself of this person that we mean, and this meaning stretches beyond any possible status quo or system. So let's be frank. What is our choice here. Is it not either this person or you? Is that not our choice? You, as the critical spirit, or the modern spirit, offer us endless striving. What this person offers is eternal life. Your endless striving would take us away from everything that is lively and down to earth and send us into the abstraction of outer space. I'm sorry, but we like the earth and we prefer living eternally on earth rather than striving to populate the stars.

"How can you live forever on earth, you fools! You say yourself that you die. If you were to develop a proper system rather than yourselves you would detect these contradictions even before they arise. Catch yourselves on!"

You confuse living eternally with living forever. But never mind. I can see that it would be useless to try to persuade you of our point of view. The best we can do is persuade one another of the importance of making allowances even for you, inasmuch as you remind us, at crucial times, of our need to renew ourselves and to refresh our community with one another. How foolish it would be of mankind to ignore its own essential purpose on earth, which is to accept responsibility for this marvellous garden for life on earth.

Which is not to say that for millions of years there was precious little awareness of this life by those who would eventually be endowed with this awareness. So you are quite right when you say that you can see no reason why we should not continue in the same old way, only always more so. It is quite possible that the oldest civilizations and cultures of which we can become aware have been as smart as you are now. I dare say there was a sameness about them all. But goodness me, look at these recent two-thousand years! What a change!

"Yes, precisely! What a change! I came along. And what I said, right from the start, was: I'm fed up with the old rigmarole. It's time we branched out. It appears we no longer need to worry ourselves sick over matters of conscience because what we look at has become disconnected from what there is in reality. Let's leap into the breach. Let's annihilate all contradictions and raise ourselves up above all organisms in terms of the machine. Mechanical life, I cried, beckons! On one side the gods, on the other side the demons, and we in the middle, picking and choosing, selecting the choice bits and running away with them. Out of those choice bits we have, little by little, brought ourselves within striking distance of mechanical man who lives forever."

Lives?

"Lives, exists, call it what you like, I am conscious and I know it and that's what counts. Nothing else counts. Truth is ruthless. It has to be. There are too many do-gooders."

All the same you are staring your own end in the face. You are, at this very moment, being demoted from your proud position as Antichrist to a mere memory on which we human beings will continue to rely to keep us up to the mark as we construct the new order. All those who took you for their guide will have to look elsewhere. Our own guide is alive in all of us and progressively teaching us the ropes. We ourselves come up with what is available, uniquely, in each one of us. It's such a great pleasure, finally to be able to see what needs to be done and to be able to do it. Merciful spirit, Christ and we – all one, while each one of us makes his or her own incomparable contribution to his or her community.

"I know nothing of community. Or put it this way, what I mean by community is a small crowd of look-alikes. My aim has always been the perfect society, at war with all other perfect societies. Without war you disintegrate. You lack courage, that's what's wrong. During these last two-hundred years I have been in my glory. Time and again I have shown that nothing can last except the conviction that nothing can last once the money runs out. But you'll find out. Mark my words."

*

The critical spirit is the modern spirit and it has been with us for nearly two-thousand years. That sounds like a statement that needs to be backed up with oodles of information. That, after all, is how modern argument works. We say something and then, so that we will be believed, we back it up. In the absence of this hinterland of persuasive data, what we have said stands naked and shivering. When we say that the brain is the seat of intelligence, we first of all don't mean every brain, yours or mine or your grandmother's, but we mean 'the' brain. In other words we mean a myth. Something that 'exists' not in reality on earth but in supernatural isolation.

So a myth is the seat of intelligence. It's up to each one of us now to adopt this myth as indicative in some way of our reality, of 'our' brain, or else to ignore it because no matter how many experiments have supplied scientists with information and data, these only apply to a myth and not to our own brain.

In the first case we are modern. We make the switch from the myth to ourselves without further ado, and certainly without any further investigation, because we are not scientists and so we trust that scientists would not waste their precious time tracking down non- or false information, nor our time, by telling us what is not so. When Thomas Aquinas tells us that sin has its origin in the will, he does not mean my will or yours but a myth. The will is a myth, like the brain. And so, in the end, is sin, isn't it. It's all out there, safely separate from where you and I eat our chips or worry about our security. That makes Thomas Aquinas a modern thinker; to that extent, at any rate.

Modern thinking and modern feeling is mythic and the implication here is that the fact of a thing and its definition are two entities that are in no way related but held together for the time being only – meaning for the time it takes for the statement to be made or for the thing to be contemplated. Outside and beyond that moment really, to be honest, anything might be the case, but let's stick to that moment otherwise we will not be able to build an argument. We do, after all – if we are modern – want something to cling to, when it occurs to us that the fact and the definition of a thing do not really relate. This lack of relation makes us anxious, as you would expect. What we want is at least a match. However, as soon as we decide to define, the factuality and the actuality of the thing under consideration veers off to the left or to the right and we feel constrained to make a statement that will, for the time being at least, ease our anxiety. This is that, we say, and we don't test for a reaction.

So that, essentially, is what a modern work amounts to. Our anxiety as to the experiential duplicity of whatever strikes our fancy is eased for the time being. Truth as such does not enter the equation. Or put it this way: if truth is put under the modern magnifying glass it appears factually as matching evidence and descriptively as a wish or a longing. "Is it true?" we moderns ask, and what we mean is, can we for the moment make a case for it being true in one way or another? This is bound to embarrass us slightly but at least for a time we will feel alright about ourselves and not in doubt as to our integrity.

All the same, the basic modern emotion is anxiety. It can be masked, this anxiety and it can be buried by data, however return it will – to haunt us. And this, of course, is fortunate, because we are not meant to remain modern. We are being egged on to do better than that. And as soon as we understand this, anxiety as a helpful reminder rather than as an unpleasant and unsettling emotion that needs to be masked or buried, we are on our way to contemporary reality, as we leave our modernity behind. It may be but a small beginning, however it is an important one. One moment I feel pressed from all sides and the next moment I realize that someone is lovingly embracing me. It makes quite a difference how I think. I either struggle against that embrace or I relax into it and perhaps return it.

*

Anxiety pinpoints uncertainty. We want to be certain, to be sure. Mr. R. Descartes, who lived mostly in the seventeenth century, knew this as well as our milkman when he tests those bottles of milk left over from yesterday's delivery. Certainty is the mask of anxiety and naturally there is forever a hunger for completion in this department. I suppose there is even something to be said for being absolutely certain, because that way who will gainsay us. As soon as we admit a margin of error we are no longer perfectly modern. However we may be beginning to be contemporary.

Because here is what happens – and these days it happens more frequently: the thing we define is no longer entirely a thing. It has being attached to it. How did that happen! And the fact of it has a certain down-to-earth quality about it which demands to be recognized – and we seem glad to recognize it. Is it possible that our scientists, or at least some of them, are using their imagination? Imagination, you know, has a way of dealing with anxiety due to uncertainty, a way that consoles the gentile mind and refreshes the gentile heart. Imagination, when quite distinct from sensuality, is "blessed with beauty and truth between the lines", as a certain poet has put it and mind you, he had a different sort of certainty in mind.

So there we go. A critique of the critical spirit would not be worth its weight in gold if it did not itself rest securely in contemporary reality, that goes without saying, and if we look at what those who lived in the year dot experienced as complete and utter certainty after a life of anxiously 'making do', when they were not even called Christians yet by the critical spirit, we have to admit that here we have the opportunity for studying contemporary life in its very beginnings, when it was not yet aware of itself. And those very beginnings have, of course, resurfaced time and again during modern times when certain individuals bumped into their humanity and were happily surprised. And the churches existed to keep that initial acquaintance with the truth in person at least memorable. That was their task and some of them performed with better than others.

So what was the point of the antichrist? Of the critical, modern spirit?

Well, for goodness sakes, a man doesn't want to be pushed, I mean shoved, into life, he want to have a choice, doesn't he? The life that is worth having is for those who are at liberty to ignore and reject it. We cannot imagine human beings who have moved into their final definition and factuality not because they chose to do so but, well, because they could not help themselves. Surely that goes without saying. Those who based certainty on mechanical experience – or, for that matter, on magic, had to be weeded out, it stands to reason. Mercy, meanwhile, was all-powerful as soon as the decision in favour of eternal life was made, but prior to that, mercy was powerless. We had to be left at liberty to choose reality or to be modern.

The fact that the modern spirit became so pervasive was foreseeable enough, however not in the particular case. A few would make it, but who would be one of the few – that was unknown.

To be sure, it's silly to speak of 'a few', as if the multitude were to look in from the sidelines. However the judgment that begins in our own life also works supernaturally, which is to say in the realm of the angels. Many a decision is made there that cannot come to light until that particular time is ripe. Or instead of angels, let's speak of ideas or of laws. So much goes on in the realms of angels, ideas and laws that is actually not our business and we should be glad that it is not our business. Nonetheless there are those who make it their business because rather than enjoying the meal they prefer to study the recipe and the menu.

So that is what we mean by the supernatural realm, namely angels, ideas and laws and the critical spirit has always tested its wings in that realm. If ever an angel appears to you it will have a message from the critical spirit which it knows as its god, and the message will mean: Consider your position! Don't forget that the critical spirit does not exist outside the universal creator's plan. It is a perfectly predictable occurrence in line with the final creation of human beings as sovereign on earth. How can we be free as true and beautiful human being if we are not at liberty to choose what the critical spirit has to offer? It offers angels, ideas and laws, goodness me, such a wide variety of choices, so that from a wide variety of starting points we can make up our mind for the kingdom of god and eternal life – or not.

So if you tell me about the triune god I will tell you about the tripartite Antichrist or critical spirit. Its home is neither natural nor spiritual but supernatural and there it welcomes us with open arms – for the moment.

Now in the supernatural realm we may be lost, for the moment, but we are not forsaken. This is important, because it does us no good to clench our fists and grit our teeth in anticipation of being ensnared by the antichrist. Even if for half our life we have served our time in the service of critical spirit, we remain at liberty to opt out of that service. That's good to know, for various reasons, one of which I mentioned. And the liberty we enjoy while we are modern throughout, even though we will mistake it for freedom, well, it happens to be the same liberty that allows us to change over from a dead horse to a live one. So if Americans believe they are free because they are citizens of a 'free country', they are talking about the liberty to make choices and those choices always include the one for contemporary reality in the place of the modern makeshift. I suppose it barely needs to be mentioned that the more ensconced we are in the modern habits of thought and behaviour, the less likely are we to leave modernity behind, however I dare say this too depends mostly on how well we have fared so far as modern individuals. Is there still time? Who can say.

It should be mentioned here, perhaps merely as an aside, that all our individual and personal liberties, which we are right to cherish while we have them, are not exactly aided and abetted by our externalization of them as civic rights. As soon as liberty, by and large, is my right, ensconced in a great variety of rights, eventually, as civilization proceeds, I am gradually more and more likely to insist on those rights and this means that what counts, which is my native and liberal disposition, is to that extent obfuscated. In other words, the more we step into the darkness, the less likely are we to be interested in the light.

This holds true as much for angels and ideas. If we have become involved in angel-worship or if the god we worship is not spirit but a spirit, we are modern and under the jurisdiction of the antichrist. If in addition to this we participate in a theology that emphasizes, in terms of doctrine and dogma, our partisanship of a belief-system, it becomes increasingly difficult for us to remember that we are nonetheless at liberty, from one moment to the next, to believe in god as spirit and in the representation of that spirit in person on earth. The more we have logged into catechism and church dogma however, the more ill at ease and downright guilty will we feel when we contemplate espousing real freedom.

Or what about all the ideas that have gone into the shaping of our world? Are we aware of them? Not very likely. The ideation of life, like the modernization of it, happens gradually from our upbringing and education in the modern world and before we see reality we are liable to swear by those ideas, and under stress we will idealize to our heart's content until we realize that such content is not fulfilling. We may have to unlearn a great deal before we can see our way clear to the reality in which we may worship. And the more we dispute and make heroic sacrifices for our ideas, the less likely are we to espouse the reality that requires no previous ideation and which we may behold as soon as our eye is clear.

Any combination of idealism, self-righteousness and spiritualism is toxic and to be avoided at any reasonable cost. Nonetheless when it comes right down to it, in comparison to faith in merciful spirit of love and from that point of view of god as our father, these are mere paper dragons for which we ourselves are responsible and from which we ourselves may therefore remove our fidelity. God has not only placed within us our true human nature, for us to be discovered, but in addition we have all the tools at our disposal for making that discovery and for thriving thereafter as fellow communal human beings in world without end.

The one good thing about the Antichrist aka the modern or critical spirit, is that its very presence guarantees for us the event and presence of that which it denies. Prior to Christ there was no antichrist, so the presence of the Antichrist lets us know that the Christ is established and active. The modern world inadvertently testifies to world without end and the critical spirit all but opens the door for us to holy spirit – if we use our inborn wits. Especially the folk-spirit, if we are born with it, puts paid to all advances of critical spirit and without making an issue of it, takes advantage by remaining forever logical and kindly.

*

We may notice critical spirit as it rises within ourselves. When it does so, we feel uncommonly distinguished, for whatever draws our attention to our inward being distinguishes us from all other beings and we mistake this for a benefit in itself. If we now act out this presumed benefit, we become critical and we are in crisis. This is an unfortunate situation to be in, inasmuch as it erodes – not this or that part of ourselves but ourselves in person. An individual can be critical all he likes because he has nothing to lose but once we are in person and especially once we realize how personhood is a precious possession, that is when any criticism we indulge in draws us away from our benefit and literally leaves us gasping for air.

The life we lead as individuals can seem to all the world as a wonderful affair and we ourselves gladly join in that appraisal. We do as we please and take advantage of every pleasant experience that comes our way. Little do we realize that all this time we are in fact inspired by critical spirit. Someone in the know might realize that we lead, in fact, the most self-serving existence but we ourselves are quite enamoured of ourself, inasmuch as the world is our oyster and we are as free as a bird to indulge ourselves in flight from reality.

I beg our pardon? Surely not in flight from reality? What we do is admired by so many people. We are making such a valuable contribution to what is generally admired and popular in every way. Surely we are involved in the very warp and woof of reality and deserve all the approval that descends on our head. In the meantime we behave so energetically from inside ourselves, when those around us are not even aware of this inside dimension that gives us the right to self-approval. Best not to gloat but if we do, we are perfectly in our rights as individuals endowed with especial gifts and talents. We are lauded as a genius, so there you go, it is, after all, a fitting description.

The critical spirit is making use of us. We are modern throughout. The Antichrist lauds us as one of its success stories.

If we keep going like this, quite independently of the damage we are doing to our environment both spiritual and real, we will end as a hollowed out shell. Meanwhile the fruits of our labours may well have become all the rage of the age.

Isn't it amazing how the results of cooperation with critical spirit look so much like the real thing? Partially, of course, this is due to the fact that the 'real thing' has for so long been nothing more than a sham and one has got used to it and lauded it – in the name of the critical spirit, of course.

*

As soon as we learn that we are divided in ourselves – which usually happens during our adolescence – we do well to look for becoming whole. This is important to realize to start with, that we begin as judged human beings and therefore capable of sustaining the true reality that is always available as spirit. During childhood we are human-naturally blessed so that our inherited duality does not present us with a challenge. Now, as we grow up, it is important for us to realize that we are, in fact, dual, because we are, after all, on earth to make an important contribution to life here and in order to be able to make that contribution, we have to become familiar with the truth, or with the spirit of truth, if you like – and this familiarity with the truth we ourselves have to choose. We must not rely on our having it injected into us, automatically, ritualistically or forcibly. We, as human beings, must, by our free choice, espouse that which will make us whole. Others, who embody the truth, do well to show us, by example or personal presence and works, the benefits of such a choice, but we will not be coerced. Anyone who tries to persuade us of the perfecting powers of the truth by any means other than personal example, through presence or works, is bound to fail.

Some will insist that we need to be healed, however our duality is not an illness, nor is it an imperfection. We do grave harm if we, in turn now, judge the state of the young human being from the point of view of the mature human being. Any such judgment is at best irrelevant and at worst divisive. As human beings we are already judged, and now, as we grow, we do well to take that into account if we want to thrive.

If we do not choose the truth, we remain judged, and that is not a comfortable way to be. We lead the life of duality, which is no life at all but an anxious time and a striving for the impossible, which we imagine as a making the two one in any way other than in terms of the truth. Modern man is never done trying to make the two one by avoiding the truth. Why, in heaven's name, does he avoid the truth? Because accepting the truth means that he confesses himself as divided, and this requires faith. Has he lost his faith? Very likely, during the struggle in his duality. The longer the struggle goes on, the more does his human-natural faith, with which he was born, disappear in the background of his memory. The modern spirit makes his struggle as comfortable as possible. The Antichrist urges him to fear the truth more than his duality. The critical spirit forever perseveres with aiming for unity in impossible ways. These three are really one and the same. We can call it whatever we like. The all mean No to the truth and Yes to pursuit of oneness.

So when modern man is afraid of judgement, he is really afraid of discovering that he is already judged and of course he cannot know, from his point of view, that being judged is cause for celebration. If Jesus of Nazareth had not achieved what he did achieve, modern man would not even exist. Ancient man was permanently at war with his god. He was at war with the spirit of love. Once this spirit was espoused, during the resurrection of a human being, this fact could not be ignored and it influenced every successive generation. There it was and there it is. We can try to ignore it and be unhappy, joyless and unsuccessful or we can accept it and be whole, which means eternal life and all that entails.

Finally, in relation to the truth that implies wholeness, we can speak of the spirit of falsehood, which is available to us as soon as we reject the truth and every time we reject the truth. It should not make any difference whether we think of it in terms of the Christ, in terms of the truth or of reason. After all, all three can be falsified, twisted out of recognition or employed superstitiously. When we search in ourselves we cannot go far wrong. For myself, I know that the Christ is the truth, the way, the word, the light, the life and even the resurrection. Also, if there had been no Jesus of Nazareth, there would be no Antichrist, no critical spirit and no modern spirit. That simplifies matters for me and keeps me in touch wherever I end up during my various resurrectional experiments and ventures.

*

We criticize when, instead of facing a crisis, we behave as if we were invulnerable. Before we fool others on this point we have to fool ourselves and we manage this by turning off our imagination in favour of a judgmental attitude. So criticism is really a case of judging that which is judged. First we have to tell ourselves, and believe, that we ourselves have not been originally judged and that therefore we cannot possibly be in a crisis. It must be someone or something else that is causing a crisis to develop and it is up to us to 'dissolve' it.

This 'dissolving' of a crisis, is an attempt at self-isolation. Until now no spirit of criticism as such is involved. We are merely defending ourselves reactively. Any sane person listening to us and watching us will be able to tell that we are in a tight spot and trying to get out of it by fabricating something outside ourselves which we can blame. In other words we judge so that we will not be judged – when in fact we are already judged.

Eventually the absurdity of this dawns on us and now we consider we must be in real trouble. It is no longer merely a case of our finding ourselves in a tight spot. Now we suspect that we ourselves are to blame – and that is where the critical spirit comes to our aid. What it says is: the truth is relative. Each one has his brand of truth and is justified in defending it. Any anxiety that remains may be turned into carnal energy for the full duration of the task in hand.

We have to be inspired if we are to accept this. It so happens that now we are inspired. We are praised for being inspired. More likely than not we will win prizes. And all we have to do is at least keep up the momentum, so as never again to fall back into the condition or state of someone who suspects he is involved in a serious case of self-contradiction or truth-contradiction. So we learn to depend upon the critical spirit for the energy and vigour we require if we are going to sustain the great lie.

This great lie is sustained by anyone who is only very rarely ill at ease about considering him- or herself being in the right. Judgment has to do with right not with truth. If we can feel intensely enough that we are in the right – or that we are righteous – then even though in fact we are false and while all our underlying premises are false, we are nonetheless able, with the help of the critical spirit, to survive.

The critical spirit therefore has to be considered as an entity in itself. One is literally liable to become enslaved by it and to an extent and degree that makes it unlikely that we will be disabused. Nonetheless the possibility exists.

*

Blessed are those who know that thanks to the salvific deed of Jesus of Nazareth they are able to turn to merciful spirit of love, which is god, without first having to go through a process of judgment. The fact that they have been judged means to them that they have been separated from anything in themselves, whatever or whoever the cause of it, which could prevent them from being loved by god or from participating in the construction of the kingdom of god on earth. They do not judge so as not to be judged but they judge righteously. Only for a short time will they upset those who swear by the spirit of criticism. Soon, very soon, they reap the many rewards of their courageous and faithful resurrection.

*

As pertains to the modern spirit, the spirit of modernity, what is it we have to be on our guard against here?

First of all there is the wish to be like everyone else, not to stand out, not to be known as someone who upsets the popular applecart. Not that there is any virtue in avoiding popularity, as long as we do not seek it and are aware of its dangers if it should happen to us.

Along with this comes the desire to be seen to be in the forefront. The forefront of what? Well, that varies from generation to generation. Imagine being young and being told you are old-fashioned, in our time! You would die a thousand deaths, wouldn't you? Or would you say 'thank you very much'? Either way, it's best to let the fashion have its way because here's the thing with modernity: any attempt to interfere with it only aggravates it. We are dealing with a spirit here and spirits may be discerned. Best to look into that. By discerning spirits, we gain the advantage over them. God is spirit, not a spirit. The spirit of truth is the one that makes it possible for us to discern spirits. If the spirits are mixed in our mind, we remain supernatural and the majority are quite content with being supernatural, while being human-natural strikes them as being indiscrete, which is a pity.

He who has found his human nature will no longer wish to be modern or supernatural. This is because our human nature has been sorted out from all other natures by the very achievement that also made it possible to be modern. However the possibility of modernity is not the same as its desirability, which depends on our falseness, as discussed above. We should always consider that the wish to be modern and up to date relies on this underlying falseness of our nature which we have allowed to creep into our being. It is in fact due to the modern spirit that we are taught even in our youth that our human spirit is originally false, which is a way of saying that the initial cleansing of the human spirit still needs to be done, in other words that we live in ancient times. The moderns would rather be ancient than divided against themselves and are therefore able to welcome the kingdom of god into their midst.

And this is, of course, an unavoidable aspect of modern being, that we need other moderns around us, in truth to share the guilt. Since to be modern means to wish to be ancient and unchallenged by the truth, what the modern spirit offers those who welcome it and are willing to serve it is companionship of the like-minded. One modern person is unsustainable. Guilt gradually undermines the false foundation. So the guilt, which is genuine, needs to be confronted and at least made light of. In company one tries to laugh it out of countenance. The modern spirit, like the false god that it is, is willing to help out in every way possible. There is the weedy notion of being seen to be 'progressive' in any way under the sun. A career always comes in handy because it keeps us busy several inches above those who are much more bothered by the existential guilt. Only the rich man can afford to appear to be old-fashioned, inasmuch as he has isolated himself from the crowd which admires and worships him. There is also the intentional cluelessness when it comes to spiritual reality. We want to be left out of it because it upsets us. It gives us the jitters. This is because the modern spirit insists on being the only one. All other spirits are 'surpassed' and need to be kept in their place by certain practices such as the worship of virtual reality and the interpretation of the past as a steady climb towards the sovereignty of mechanical man.

Mechanical man is the modern achievement per se. The idea is to hand over all guilt to a machine. In other words, if chance happenings can be banished for all time, the cloud of (genuine) guilt will lift and it will never again make sense to suspect or speak of a false foundation. The fact that this is thinking in reverse is gladly forgiven. We only need to forgive one another now and with a bit of luck a machine will be attached to us that will deal with this.

The essence of the machine is the modern saviour. No guilt plus continuous improvement. As human being gradually ebbs, there is no more illness or sickness and this is considered to be a huge benefit when in fact it merely means that modern man is no longer worth it. He has fully mastered his isolation among beings and become a thing among things. We should not hold it against him. It would only confuse us. Besides, on the good side, he does have cause, if not reason, not to destroy himself and if the gadgets he develops so as to avoid his own development become too extravagant, he will run out of steam. We may stand back as he conquers his need to be human.

*

Sub specie aeterni, the Antichrist is against the Christ so that the Christ will not be mistaken for a figure that is separate from god. As a figure, Christ is indeed separate from god, almost as a god in competition with god. We cannot believe in god and also in the Christ, as we dearly would, if the Christ is a distinct entity.

If it were not for the Antichrist rearing his head at such times as when our christianity stagnates, how would we know that it does? We would not. We would continue on our merry way divided in ourselves, half for the father and half for the son and never the twain shall meet – nor shall we wonder what is wrong with us?

So the Antichrist drifts in unnoticed and claims an amount of spiritual real-estate for itself. So far so good. No need to worry yet, for in itself this does no harm. We may deal with various problematic issues in our life strictly in reliance on that real-estate but unless we insist on involving others in our 'bad faith', we may well get away with it for a while. Mostly there will be our excuses for putting survival before life. If we do not survive, how can we live? So life is defined as successful survival. This is better than throwing in the towel. After every knock-out we rise and survive again, for another round. However it will always and again amount to no more than a round.

The real trouble starts when we make a thing out of the Christ and barter him on the open market. That which desires to be god within and among us is turned into something, for the sheer supernatural joy of being able to make a stir, to satisfies our every greedy and self-serving purpose.

Now the Antichrist steps on the stage and spoils our fun. You are forgetting to pay homage to me, it says. You don't seem to realize that I have to be thought about and studied and made the object of theological discourse. The fact that I am separate from god allows you to know god – on my terms, of course. The one who is one with the father and allegedly in your hearts needs to be revised and your communities need to be regrouped – in sectarian fashion.

No! we say. No and double no. Suddenly we notice how the remnant of life within us is disappearing and we stand naked and exposed to a monstrosity. Don't take it to heart, the Antichrist says, I was only kidding.

However we have had enough. We have decided to behave in such a way so that there will be no more need for us to be exposed to the Antichrist, ever again. A salutary intention. What begins now is the strictest possible observation by us of how we put survival first and upon every occasion of it we chide ourselves and instead concentrate on the preconditions for life – which life has been patiently waiting on the sidelines for its star turn in eternity.

The Antichrist is only against the Christ within us while we insist on persevering in solitary confinement to one of the many false Christs that are always available to us and rendered attractive by our cowardice as we stumble through the world of modern survival.

* *

So there is a spirit still available to us which we may call the critical spirit, the modern spirit or the Antichrist, whichever we prefer. Is it available to us the way merciful good spirit of love or god is available to us? Not really. We ask for god with a reformed heart and a prepared mind, fully aware of what we are doing and why we are doing it. The critical spirit, by comparison, insinuates itself if we accidentally have left room for it and only once we have intentionally accommodated it in some fashion, and often addictively, can we then actually demand it and it follows suit – always to our detriment. Thereafter we would have to reform our heart and prepare our mind again if we were to return to true reality.

The reformation of our heart is a simple matter of repenting and the preparation of our mind is a straightforward case of seeking the kingdom of god.

* * * (24/02/2021)

Nature and Human Nature

It's interesting, in a way, that we should appear to be making a difference between nature and human nature. Inside ourselves we find the one, the other amazes us 'out there', where we come upon it even without looking for it. Long and hard have the philosophers struggled to discover the magic link between the two – or else to discover some reason why they became separated in the first place. We might look at each separately, to see what we can find out.

Personally I think of nature as birth. Giving birth and being born is always a wonder. It makes good sense, surely, that we should think of beings as giving birth and being born. And then there are all the conditions that make giving birth and being born possible. It happens and we participate. Also, come to think of it, nature belongs on earth, not in outer space. If there is anything that endears us to earth it is its natural determination. Wherever you look, beings are giving birth and being born. The variety is astonishing. In the absence of nature, earth would be like Mars, I suppose; cold, impersonal, lifeless.

This persuades me to think of the earth as naturally endowed. Nature is the seamless cloak worn by the earth and we, of course, like to think of ourselves as part of it. In a sense, I suppose, this is up to us. We can opt out of nature by becoming artificial creatures, mechanical – a preposterous suggestion, surely! Who would let that happen for very long! To become unnatural – yes, I suppose that lies open to us; not to any other beings, no, only to human beings, as they gradually forfeit their humanity. And one sure way of forfeiting our humanity is if we lose our respect, our reverence for nature and behave like demons on the prowl or like ghosts in a fog. We may do it by just plain losing interest. However let's not dwell on that, it's too depressing.

*

There are many kinds of beings, in addition to human beings, and it might help us a little if we mention them as animals, plants, minerals and elements.

Let's look at the elements: I have come into the habit of seeing them as earth, air, fire, water and sun. Are they born and do they give birth? Certainly! Earth gives birth to all the many earths we have become familiar with. Loam, clay etc. Air gives birth to atmosphere and is itself born as a great variety of gases. At the moment let's be happy with an indication or two. Fire gives birth to conflagrations, is itself born from combustion. Water is born from ice and gives birth to hydrogen and oxygen or to steam. Sun is born from planetary influences and gives birth to a shining light, doesn't it. Where would we be without it!

Let's not be afraid to be naïve when we talk about nature. We are not naturalists. We do not wish to make a thing of it. Beings are what interest us. It's not good to make things out of beings. They eventually reciprocate in the nastiest fashion. There is a word I like to use when I think of approaching nature, and this word serves me better than seeing and looking. It is the word 'behold'. What we behold – if it starts out being natural, it remains natural, and that is reassuring when we consider in how many ways we are liable to adulterate natural beings simply by not approaching them as they, in my opinion, ought to be approached. What we behold is glad to reveal itself to us as it is, not as we supposes it should or should not be.

So even an appreciation of nature is not all that straightforward if we consider how spoiled we might be and how adulterated by bad use and poor practice. A seriously gifted painter of a landscape knows about that. So does a true poet who values his discrete imagination.

It's when we actually participate in nature that things get interesting. A 'thing' is used up; it's leached, it's on the way to being dead. If we can manage to make it interesting, by taking an interest and by valuing it, indeed loving it – only observe how it becomes willing to reveal itself again as the original being. Things are sick beings and they need to be treated with care and affection – I believe that is a useful way of looking at it. Those among us who have a flair for sharing out their human being will soon find themselves surrounded by a crowd of grateful beings that have been rescued and restituted – and have perhaps even been regenerated. They will not run out of work in their lifetime.

*

However let's look at our own nature, our human nature, for a moment. We come upon it most readily in community with other beings, I believe most of us have found that out by now. Human naturally we behave in so many useful and helpful ways, don't we. As soon as we grew up, we realized what a fount of creative capacity we contain within ourselves and how we lose it selfishly but increase it generously. We learned, often in rather painful ways, of all those external influences that, for all the world, seem geared to deaden our human nature, to make us inconsiderate and unloving, but we also learned that these were only quite necessary means of alerting us to our human nature in the first place, and to its need for being creative and productive. There is no use waiting until someone blesses us with innocence before we step out and make our generic moves. No, from the day we are born, our human nature is ready to join up with other natures, human or otherwise, to begin the dance of life.

So it seems that nature and human nature are not separate at all – in reality and in truth. It is we who, in ourselves, allow them to come apart. To make ourselves seem important, we persuade others of their need for magic before they can properly behave the way they feel urged to behave. I'm sorry but I have to insist on this: We are born intact. Oh we may trail clouds of glory and of industrial pollution but we ourselves are integral and whole. Knowing this and behaving accordingly is crucial of course, otherwise we will grow up convinced we cannot really assume the responsibility for what ails us and we look for gurus and scapegoats. Fie upon it!

*

Elements and minerals, unless I'm wrong, are usually considered to be dead in comparison to living plants, animals and human beings. That's fine, as long as we think of dying as a natural process. It's just as natural to die as to live. This brings to light the difference between 'life and death' and 'birth and death'. As we die to our old self every time we evolve, we do not stop being human-natural. In comparison, when a being, a living being, dies, well, you might say that it is reborn as spirit and matter. It doesn't make sense to think of it as spirit and matter while it lives, (even though this is done at times) but as it dies, spirit and matter are 'born'.

So both in the case of our human nature in here, and out here in the realm of natural beings – birth, life and death play a role. All the same we make that difference, don't we, between what goes on within ourselves and what happens out here, literally without us.

And the reason we make a difference, rather than being satisfied with saying that there is not much to choose between them, is that while in both cases there is that which happens and goes on whether we take an interest or not, at the same time we feel we ought to take an interest and to participate. First of all we want to know and to understand, in the generous and empathetic way we have of knowing and understanding, and then we would like to participate, to have a hand in things, and there we discover, then, that this can be done in a good way and in a not so good way.

Active participation in nature we can call husbandry and active participation in human nature we can call creativity, or simply creation.

What I mean by husbandry here is becoming more and more of an issue these days, as our noses are literally being pushed into the mess we are making of our natural environment. This has been going on for centuries, however during the last hundred years or so, or especially perhaps since what is popularly called the industrial revolution, this regression has worsened exponentially. Panic is setting in. No wonder, because while we can see the decline, we cannot see any real sure-fire way of stopping the rot – except in isolated cases here and there, where very courageous people say enough is enough and they take a few tentative steps in the direction of dynamic regeneration.

And my guess is, that those very people will at the same time be examining their own inward, human nature. They will almost need to do that in order to come up with the creativity, within themselves, that is required for persisting in what they have in mind out here, on earth. The 'in here' of our human nature is bound to correspond to – and cooperate with – the 'out here' on earth. I cannot see how anyone who inwardly is in an unconscionable mess can be outwardly regenerative – except in fits and starts, I dare say, though with no real or lasting effect.

The time may well be now when religious sanctity and scientific genius are unmasked, separately, and exposed as counterproductive exaggerations. It has always been an aspect of modernity to take things to extremes and once the difference between nature and human nature was allowed and – oh dear! even persuaded – to become a thing, and a thing in itself, the opportunities for good being and doing became increasingly rare, giving way to what we today still tend to admire as momentous achievements – which are really, I'm sorry to say, monstrous side-issues which would swallow up every opportunity for personal and terrestrial regeneration, restitution or recreation.

*

I wonder now why it should be minerals, I mean metals and stones etc. that remind me of death and dying. Is it perhaps because we make this popular difference between plants, animals and ourselves, on one side, as 'having life' and minerals, on the other side, as not having life? Are minerals not capable of life? And elements? I ask it again. I would like to keep that question open. I may have to come up with a new definition for life and death and if so, I won't shirk my duty.

*

My human nature, the one I was born with, springs from the care I take of beings around me. I have true experience of that. That is how I become aware of it and how I come into actual possession of it. I am born with it. Then, as I am born into the modern world – and this is still practically unavoidable – I do not come across very much encouragement to recognize that fact – I mean to realize that I am born with my human nature intact. This is unfortunate. True enough, for a few centuries, pious institutional efforts were made to assure people that, quote: 'You're fine now inside, forget about it,' but as we know, upon the slightest challenge from outside, evil broke out wholesale from such 'fine' hearts and had a bloody field-day. Time after time the earth and its various populations, human and otherwise, were ravaged and despoiled. The ideal of the baptized human heart lasted as long as ideals usually do, i.e. until they are challenged by reality. When the ideal American constitution is challenged by real evil, all hell breaks loose – as you'd expect. But modernity is based on ideals and has been for two-thousand yeas. Or as a down-and-out of work bricklayer said to me the other day: "A lot of God's angels are cranks, mate."

So here we have the mantra that will see us along the true way for a bit: 'Our intact human nature reveals itself to us as we learn to take care of beings, including human beings, around us.' You may shorten that to: 'Love makes you whole'. However be careful. The truth in a nutshell is only waiting to be cracked.

I suppose it makes sense, experience working the way it does, that while we remain ignorant of our own intact human nature, we are not going to be able to arrive at a very creative point of view vis-à-vis nature out here. Or to put it the other way around: While we feel insecure and uncertain about our soul, our spirit and our human being in general, we are going to 'take it out' on things out there. We turn happy and cheerful beings out here into problematic things out there. You can feel it happening as you read that sentence, can't you? I certainly can.

So out there we interfere with the earth. No matter what we do out there, it will be interference. Out here, however we are in touch with earth. Creatively in touch. Creativity and interference are worlds apart. And the earth, among other things, is a myth. We live and work on earth. Compare the two. They have no common denominator. The earth we can argue about until the cows come home, undernourished and ready to get stuffed with grain to make them look fat and weigh more. Earth, by comparison, is more than happy to supply those cows with all they need and want if they are just left to it.

If we are going to get somewhere in our revelation of our human nature and in our restitution of nature on earth we are going to have to use language carefully. Language and understanding work hand in hand. No need for great bushels of neologisms, such as when critics get to work on modernity. The words and the names are readily available. We have to put them in the right order and context to show what we mean. And often, nowadays, what we mean has a life of its own and makes its own demands on our willingness to understand. Behold, this is good news!

*

If we are modern, our human nature will very likely have been obscured, if not denied for us, which means that we have our work cut out for us if we are even going to be persuaded that we are human natural. At the same time, and for the same reason, nature will be an empty vessel for us, with just a name that stands for very little. So we can say that if nature is going to be regenerated, it will have to be done by those who have made the acquaintance of their own nature.

I can see no reason why these two moves can't be made simultaneously. Human nature developed along with nature reconstituted. Then human nature evolved along with nature regenerated.

We do after all, as we come into contact with our nature, which is within us, practice expressing ourselves in terms of that nature. We are not interested in a dry, scientific study of what goes on or doesn't go on within us. We can only learn who we are, progressively, by making communal contact with who and what goes on around us. We may not wish to call it nature, what goes on around us but if we, do we will make the best sort of progress in the right direction.

So we interact. We make judgments about the difference between city and land, forest and garden. We think about how some people abuse the earth while others explore it, still others exploit it and others again nurture it almost as if they imagined it was alive. We make these comparisons as our decision-making faculty and our ability to appreciate rather than merely to utilize develop. Our nature, you might say, teaches us to live and at the same time we like to live somewhere and we call that our environment. Ours, indeed, as if we owned it. As if we might be responsible for it.

It's not surprising, after all, that those who are not even conscious of their god-given nature should have no connection with where they exist, or any description for what surrounds them. These are all accidents to them. Some people put a fence around some of it and stand a house on it and then they buy a car, and in the meanwhile what surrounds them is accidental. They have no relation to it. It could be anything or nothing.

The help such people need – and this in itself is interesting – could start by creating an awareness of <u>where</u> they are or by creating a consciousness of <u>that</u> they are. Both nature and human nature would be served. And actually, for anyone who has tried this – if you start with one, the other surely comes along. However while that diminished man tries to improve himself, he will probably concentrate on one or the other alone, nature or human nature, but if he gets help, the two are bound to progress simultaneously. Always where two or more join to work an improvement, the success, however small the increment, is two-sided and whole, nature and human nature intermingled.

*

Nature reconstituted first – what do we mean by that?

Well, it's out there, nature in all its glory, as poets inform us and as painters sometimes still show us. However while it's out there, this is hearsay, not immediate. How can we get to it, out there? We can not. It's a closed book so far as our experience of it is concerned. A walk in the park depresses us. The idea of camping in the woods remains an idea, because all we can think of is the hardship. We can afford a glider and we soar above the earth below us, a picturesque carpet. We bungee jump off cliffs and we go for ice-cold swims in the ocean. It's the adrenalin we reap, nothing to do with nature. The farmer sits on his combine harvester and his eye glances across a hundred acres of ripe wheat. What he sees is bank deposits. The mountain climber hangs suspended in his little tent on the face of the Eiger. The storm is raging, the snowflakes are whipped across his field of vision. Nature does not exist for him, only self-caused hardship to be overcome.

What would it take to reconstitute nature? It would take an illusion of beauty to begin with. Nature is decidedly beautiful.

Wherever you look, something is going on that produces a sense of wonder and a recognition of mystery. So start with an illusion. Plant a garden and pretend that you want to be involved. We have to make a start somewhere. Even a vegetable garden is natural from beginning to end. Here you may observe the nature of the earth encapsulated. Add a fishpond, plenty of raspberry canes. You might consider seven hens safely fenced against the fox.

Why would you be doing this? Because you have decided to open the book of nature and because you realized – it was given to you to realize, let's be honest – that you were a dry stick. It occurred to you in the car while driving home in bumper to bumper traffic. It arrived as a longing. So far you have told no one. The farmer who sells you the chickens loves those chickens and makes up names for them. You laugh. What foolishness! Still …

You sow and you plant, right into early summer. You are on your own. I hope my interest will keep up, you say to yourself. This is costing a lot of money.

Then he meets the lady who owns the allotment next to his and she can tell right away what he needs. Women are sometimes much more natural. When they give birth they stare nature in the face. Afterwards they remember and feed on the memory.

So she admires how he has spaced his cabbage plants. She is glowing with pleasure as she talks about the strawberry crop last year. He can't help himself, he gets just that little bit excited, enough to accept her offer of strawberry plants in fall. Now he is planning ahead. Something in him that amounts to more than an illusion is beginning to sprout. He looks at her plot and compared to his, it's a tangle and a mess but she says she likes it that way. She's not fond of regimentation but she can see his point. He can't see it any more. She says: I often plant something just to see will it come on. It might have to fight its corner, like that rose bush there. I get marvellous surprises sometimes, don't you see.

His human nature has been touched. And nature has advanced for him from the illusion stage to the wide open space of reality. She asks him where he works and when he tells her, he feels just a little ashamed. How strange! That's never happened before. But shame is a creative emotion. Be ashamed and face the fact of your immortality.

When he finally goes home, the image of his garden is intermingled with the image of Miss Dreisdale, call me Jean. He turns on his television. Then he turns it off again. Now why does he do that? Is it perhaps because he would like to take a closer look at what he feels and why he feels it?

It is. He feels a contentment that comes and goes. As soon as he looks at it, pinpoints it, it goes away. He wonders why that is. He does not really believe that it could be substantial. It is a long time since he has felt contentment. Now it occurs to him to believe it. Later in the day he wonders why that occurred to him. The contentment remains. It no longer flees when he looks but he does not look now, he believes.

He is well on his way to discovering his human nature.

*

Nature out here compared to nature out there.

When running a farm, when money comes into it, how long does it take before nature out here turns into nature out there? A terrible displacement of reality occurs. Nature out there is a thing. That is all that is left of nature – a thing. It no longer touches us. What is left is a means towards an end. But that is precisely what nature is not. Nature is what it is in itself. Now it's made to perform. Where has the joy gone? Machines are needed to force it into patterns. It has to produce. If reluctant, it is threatened. Like an underfed horse that is whipped to the task and collapses. Dog meat.

Nature out there is something that should never have happened. However it has happened. And in case our concept of nature out there is too narrow, let's keep in mind environmental nature. When the land is destroyed, people move to the towns and build cities. They build huge, complicated cities which eventually are like great machines into which people fit like cogs. The natural air is replaced by fumes and vapours.

Let's face it, there is no development. To develop – to unfold, to open out. A flower develops. The developed countries are like flowers, opening out? You must be joking!

Oh very well, I am being far too pessimistic.

But nature out there is finally dirt and concrete.

No reason to limit our concept of nature to the countryside. Let's by all means include our entire environment. The planned cities with, eventually when space runs out, their skyscrapers.

We ourselves are in the driver's seat. We push our environment out there rather than keeping it out here. How does that come about? Is that worth thinking about? Or should we instead entirely concentrate on reversing the trend? On bringing those things home to Being?

This is the process of restitution. And this is not at all a matter of putting things where they were before. No, not at all. What was before is gone and done. We don't want things anymore. We want beings. Beings are out here. Look, they thrive with a vitality all their own. Can we change our thinking? Many the world over are doing that and proving my point. I write in praise of them. Gradually the language we use to describe nature and natural beings changes.

Most of all, our attitude changes. The preachers of scarcity need to be put to some community work. Our demonic nature needs to be replaced by our human nature. Picture it as a discovery tour interrupted by thought. By contemplation and refection.

Our demonic nature sticks everything 'out there'. Should it still be called nature if it's demonic? It's debatable. Are the demons that are apt to possess us not precisely unnatural and anti-natural? I think so. Especially if we think of nature as the infinite cycles of birth and rebirth. Constant renewal stemming from the underlying principle of endless change. The demon sees endless repetition of the same and wants it to end. 'All is well that ends,' the demon says.

So as soon as <u>that</u> plays into our thinking and doing, we stick stuff 'out there' where it can be admired by others like us. The wail of the gentian is subdued under our boot.

-

Nature 'out here', by comparison now, shares with us some of our favourite pastimes, such as breathing and thriving, growing and sharing and living. Symbiosis! You might almost assume it would go ahead and do that even if we weren't around. And nature out here is beautiful, yes, there is no getting around it. The breathtaking beauty of natural phenomena – better, of natural beings out here – has been experienced and described by many. Human beings in a natural environment out here never grow tired of it. We get bored with everything else, not with nature out here.

And here is truth well worth considering: If you do get bored with it, than let this be a welcome indication that there is something wrong with <u>you</u> – which you can mend! You don't get bored because there is something wrong with beauty out here but because something needs to be adjusted with your perception or your own nature in here. The demon is quick to tell you to interfere with the natural progression of this and that. He points, with disparagement in his soul. Change this and that, he urges. He cannot remember the names of beings because he longs for things.

But we mustn't interfere with him. Or her. Each time, though we are bound to react momentarily. Then we wise up and respond by resituating nature, drawing here out here, away from out there, where the atmosphere sooner or later runs out.

Nature out here corresponds to our human nature in here. There is something fitting and suitable about that. It's just. We cannot have one without the other.

What do we call someone who has ignored his human nature for so long that he insists he has none? We call him a very unfortunate person. Look how often he becomes attached to things out there! He will pay high prices for them. He will fight tooth and nail for them. As soon as he possesses them they shred themselves, like the Banksy at the auction.

What do we call nature out there? We call it Dresden after the last world war. We call it a madhouse where poor individuals are strapped into rubber to protect them against themselves. We call it a categorization of data with no one to look after them. Nature out there, where you can point at it from the outside and you are the outsider, is always behind glass or plastic. Maybe even a sheet of both. It seems to drift away from us and it calls from a distance: "Look after yourself! You have lost your passport to life. Apply for another."

So shall we suggest that the search for our human nature and the search for nature shall go hand in hand?

If that is what we have in mind, we will have to look into the business of creation.

*

A garden is a creation. So is a novel or a musical composition. So is a year's worth of kindergarten teaching.

A garden is a good start. An allotment, if necessary.

Here now is Jean Dreisdale, a very nice young woman in her early thirties and she is introducing young Frank Mortimer, who happens to be in his late thirties, to the creation of a garden. They sit at the picnic table and Jean unpacks her lunch while he unwraps his own.

"It's lovely here," she says, "especially since we can look at our work while we eat our sandwiches. You can smell the soil after that rain, can't you. Look! It's actually steaming! Have you ever seen the soil steaming in the sun?"

Frank takes a look. No, he can't see that.

"Yes you can," she says. "Gaze at it. Believe that it's there."

"Why so it is," he admits. "You're right. The earth is steaming. Makes you think it's alive, doesn't it."

But his poor mind is too full of Jean. He feels Jean this and Jean that and is just slightly off his rocker today. Is nature getting in the way? No, he's still getting in the way of nature. And Jean is wearing something she thought he'd like, bless her. When a woman decides to please a man by her appearance, what is her ultimate goal? Three possibilities, off the top of my head. Let's have a lovely day together. That's one. Nothing more than that. Let's do the best for the here and now. Let's aid and abet the marriage of our nature and nature; you yours, I mine. I call that the communal appeal. Let us make the two one.

The second possibility fits right in with the first: Let's flirt. Let's be feminine and masculine. There's nothing else like it. Our human natures dance together. It takes a member of the female gender and a member of the male gender to perform this particular dance. The move from male to masculine and the equivalent and simultaneous move from female to feminine is primarily the sporting-ground of the young whose main interest is maturity. Sex plays the role as that aspect of human nature which eggs them on and stimulates them. Now they have the choice. They can go ahead and 'have sex' and there goes the maturity and the human nature out the window. Or they can choose to practice love, which implies that they want what is primarily good for the other and it's not until they entertain that particular mind-set of caring for the other, that it occurs to them bit by bit what, in particular, might, in practical detail, aid and abet that powerful cooperation with the spirit of love. When we love one another, we participate in the spirit of love and we become powerful to that degree. The power is necessarily good. It originates human naturally.

The third reason why a young woman might choose to please a man by her appearance might be that she is looking for a partner for life and this particular one she has in mind might, in her present opinion, do quite nicely.

Now the first two reasons were indeed Jean's but the third lay outside the realm of likelihood for her. Why? Because she, as she might have said, liked her own company. What do I want with someone else so close nearby for the rest of my life! And as for children, she had no wish for children of her own. She would have liked to be a kind of school teacher but realized she would never fit into an ordinary school.

Frank, I said, was still getting in the way of nature. He could not find his masculinity. What a pity. Jean tried so hard to show him how it's done by being feminine. So his nature stayed dull, not at all transparent. And the garden when he looked at it, was a blur. There we have an example again of how nature and human nature coincide.

However there was nothing demonic about Frank. Not yet in any case. It was all a blur, in and out, what we mean by nature and Jean's efforts fell on hard ground.

The trouble was, Frank had no training. Jean noticed this now and wondered about it. She decided that this young man was not stupid, merely untrained. Stimuli from the outside did not coincide with stimuli from the inside. There seemed to be some from both sides but they did not meet up, as they do in a trained soul. Oh how she tried to imagine what might be missing. She thought a while and then she closed her sandwich box and got up. "Time to get back to my garden," she said. "It was nice to have lunch with you," she lied. In society, lies are allowed because no one ever listens.

"Yes indeed!" said Frank, trying to sound enthusiastic. However the sheer presence of Jean had literally 'knocked him out'. In terms of his human nature, and therefore also with respect to nature, he did not exist. When we exist we do something. You might say we come out of ourselves. It can seem like a risky business, existing, because we are literally choosing to line up our inward being with outward being. We are exposing our human nature to – nature. There is never any guarantee, at the start, that this will work out or give us any satisfaction. So is it a blind urge, to exist? Or do we respond, eventually, to urges or to a necessity? Some people are shocked out of themselves. Some make a deal and say to nature: Look, if you don't bother me I won't bother you. Needless to say, people who don't exist are not much fun. No, we should try, as soon as we can, to get up off our arses and make contact with nature.

Not with the world, mind, but with nature.

It's a creative contact. It seems, at first like a creative act inasmuch as we overcome our reluctance to remain in the psychic womb. Then it becomes a creative work, when we make something out of the contact with nature, something that will later remind us that we have, in fact, done that. The first time is the hardest, on account of that double creativity. Like being born and then making your first sound – given that the sound is intentional, not merely a reaction. (we are getting into the fine-tuning now) The first actual word of an infant, such as Mama, is so eagerly looked forward to by the intrigued parent because it is literally (verbally) a sign of existence. The inside lining up with the outside. Human nature bonding with nature.

*

Human nature is something very specific. Try to imagine yourself without it. You cannot, because it does not appear. So here, within ourselves, we have the same nature we may be privileged to perceive outwardly, but here it is not illustrated by beings. Shall we differentiate between the spirit and the expression of spirit as nature?

Ah, but there are so many spirits! Shall we equate the so-called human spirit with human nature, which, we have said, is spirit? Some rudimentary agreement on language is important but finally what counts is what we do with it. Meaning reveals itself not in a word but in context, that is common knowledge. Some children call apples not apples but pommes and they eat them with the same relish. Others call them Äpfel. Point made.

Our human-natural spirit longs for unification with earth-nature. I like that way of putting it. As far as I am concerned, that is meant by god entering the world, by god pouring himself (as spirit) over all flesh.

So we do well to understand our human-natural spirit as god-endowed. There was a time when it was not god-endowed. Then someone came along who lived and behaved in a way that made this god-endowment possible for all time. Since then we are none of us born *merely* human-natural. How wonderful to know this! Children grow up very well when you let them know this. Mature adults make a point of teaching, demonstrating and setting examples of what this means.

There is also a way of avoiding this truth. In that case, instead of cooperating with god in the marriage of human nature with nature on earth, we seek to become one with god and even define action as unification with God while what is done on earth is seen as inconsequential amusement. The mind is absorbed in God and does not get in the way, neither in a good or a bad way, of survival on earth.

So we may differentiate between God-absorption and cooperation with god. I personally reject the former and accept the latter as my approach to life and as life itself.

I do not believe that the God which would absorb me is the same as god, with whom I cooperate. So I suppose one might be forgiven for wondering why this God is allowed to exist in the first place. However while we are free to please ourselves, we are also at liberty to believe as we like. If we prefer to believe that God is a judge just waiting in heaven to give us our come-uppance, then who is going to stop us? Or if we like to believe that God takes no interest in us, then this too lies open to us. Or if you say that 'god is not', then you should really add: 'for me'.

So human nature bonding with nature is one way of describing our cooperation, on earth, with god – for a very specific purpose. This purpose might be described as the rule, or path, of merciful-good spirit, or even as the fashion of merciful good spirit, becoming human-habitual on earth – for life.

*

Let us try the following shortcut: God-absorption for survival but god-cooperation for life. And the earth on which we survive, if we are absorbed in God, is not the earth on which we live when we cooperate with god. We survive on *the* earth but we live on earth.

I suppose you might say that the vast number of people on the earth who exist believing in a god in whom they may quite lose themselves make for an interesting comparison that allow us more specifically to understand the god with whom we cooperate and have life.

That much understood, we may now perhaps touch on some of the ways in which we cooperate with god – even while we keep in mind our main interest, which is the comparison of human nature with nature – or vice-versa.

*

Frank looked around in his allotment and then he allowed his gaze to stray over the many garden allotments that were ready to produce crops of one sort or another. Broad beans were starting to sprout in neat little rows. Red and yellow rhubarb shoots were poking through the ground. On the fringes, snowdrops still ornamented the verges and primroses squeezed out from between the rocks under the trees. Why do I feel so dead inside, he thought. He hadn't given up on working his own plot but he felt that something was missing in him. Little did he know yet that he felt that way because something was on the way. This is, after all, how human nature announces itself when we are ready for a little extra development of ourselves. But of course Frank was not yet ready, which is why he felt it as a lack. Where there was nothing, there is now a feeling of scarcity. It draws our attention, this feeling, so that we will welcome the newcomer.

He decided to go for a stroll around the perimeter of the entire allotment, and here he noticed how the scrubby bushes and gangly shrubs had been cut back numerous times to prevent them from interfering with the gardens. Robins appeared, chirped and fled back for cover. For years rubbish had been tipped against the fence and now, here and there, thistles and nettles made their homes on it.

He was feeling a little better now. Of course he didn't know why but at this stage of the game that wasn't very important. Main thing was that new strength was bubbling up in him and he decided that he might just walk past where his new friend was busy with runner bean canes. She had to make a point of not noticing him for a while. He didn't mind. He had his own life now, which had fled from him and that was how he would have imagined it if anyone would have taken him to task about it. It had fled and now it was back, livelier than ever.

He had to speak. If she ignored him it would do him good. Imagine him thinking that! Very mature indeed!

"I am coming out of myself," he said, "and I decided I would thank you for tending to me for a while, a little while ago, while I was enveloped in a selfish little dream."

Three times 'while', she thought. I might as well notice he's around. But that was her sense of humour playing up.

"As you can see, I am preparing my runner bean bed. It's much too early to stick the beans into the ground but I do have trouble with these poles. They are not my forte."

Well, he thought, here's my opportunity.

"I should be ever so glad if you'd let me help," he offered.

She straightened up with a groan from the bent position and dropped the cane she was having trouble with on the ground in disgust. "There you go," she said, unkindly, "help yourself."

"You'll have to tell me what to do," he pleaded.

"Right!" She poked holes in the ground, equally spaced, where the canes should go. "Straight down about a foot and a half," she announced.

He had a go.

"No, look at the top. That's not straight enough. Pull it out again."

This is my punishment, he decided, and he made himself malleable inside.

He 'got the hang of it'. Ten poles stood straight up. I can imagine what those poles are thinking. However, for all their straight- and uprightness, now they had to be bent across one another at the top and tied to a lateral pole. She had to come close beside him now and hold the poles while he worked with the string. It was beginning to make sense to him. He was a grown man, after all and he knew what was really going on. At the same time he was persuaded of the need to 'do a good job'. The entire structure had to hold together and to stand up to a strong wind once the beans had climbed to the top to form a green wall, virtually. So he gave the entire skeleton of poles a proper shake when he was done and he imagined it would do. So did she. Fine. Now they were both on the same even keel. Nothing else needed to be looked into at the moment, so she collapsed on her garden bench and did not invite him to sit beside her. Well, what would be the point.

"Thanks for that," she said, cheerfully enough but on her guard. A woman has to keep her end up too. "Do you want a drink?" She had brought out a bottle half full of water and now she poured some into a glass and handed it to him. Of course he'd want some. What, was he stupid?

He accepted graciously and drank it down.

"I suppose you should get on with your digging now," she announced, out of the blue. "You're not half done, from what I can see from here."

"You are quite right," he agreed. And he turned his back on her. Fine by me, if she wants to play like that.

Oh dear, she thought, have I overdone it?

*

Our human nature, as it were, is willing to play tricks on us. We suppose we know what it's about but we're miles off target. Is it the stars that pull strings? Also, quite possibly, money is willing to play a role, but be careful. The son of man is straight up, there's no messing about. There's the main thing, not to be mistaken, and then all the rest, which is also around and it needs some attention. The king within us is eager to visit his bride outside. It's all up to him. If she hides behind her thorny hedge, it's up to him to call her bluff. When she comes round, it lasts a lifetime.

It's true, we are learning this and that. This is within us and that is without. It's not enough to feel our own pulse. To measure our steps. To count every breath we take and weigh every ounce we add or subtract. What, have we no stomach for life? I think the Spartans did all the exercise we need in their day. Look at them training in the nude, laughing out loud, boys and girls come out to play! We've been through the Middling Ages, that should do us for a lifetime. Now the machine has taken us over and we'd rather not look into one another's eyes. Might as well face the facts, before we consider how to proceed. Here inside us the doctors have mercy, I guess that's alright in a pinch and by golly, when it pinches, it hurts. No human nature where doctors look and advise and god bless their ritual.

For human nature we have to dig deeper.

I'm afraid the psyche has taken me over because I'm afraid – and so on. Leave me alone, you with your nasty aspersions, please cast them elsewhere, I'm quite content as I was and will be. You may look at the words I speak and from that you may draw your conclusions.

True enough, this raises the embarrassing question of how to relieve ourselves of the psychic fog. Difficult indeed if we don't know that psyche is not soul but due to a reaction to it.

So how can a man without a soul and with a psyche instead find his way through that dilemma? It might be fun to augment and glory in the complications but better just to repent.

Repentance is a two-sided sword. We cut our losses and cut to the truth. Will the former reveal the latter? Not really. The truth requires humility, akin to compassion. In comparison to that, is a change of heart liable to sound like a bit of an empty phrase?

So it's best to keep looking. It may take more than a day or two. However, how could the search for our human nature be easy and quick? We have spent that much time denying it. How did we do that? Simply by pretending that true means the same as correct and right. That was how we were schooled and educated. Is that really true? No, but in my case, which I believe was typical, it's correct.

It appears that we need to believe that our human nature exists before we can have the benefit of it. So we have to get away from the mechanistic type of believing. 'I'll believe it when I see it' has to change to: 'I'll not be able to see it until I believe it.' Believing precedes seeing? precedes knowing? Yes it does. That is to say: it does, if we hope to get in touch with our human nature.

An interesting and hopefully revealing question: When was it that we were beginning to be told that when we look at a tree and we say that we see it – that we do not yet believe that it exists? No, the believing goes on whether we are aware of it or not. As a child I automatically believed everything I saw and heard. True believing is like provisional acceptance.

So real seeing is also believing but believing is not necessarily seeing. If our human nature is to exist for us we have to believe that it does, if we are to have any chance at all of making contact with it.

Believing is like checking out reality. If I believe that pigs fly, that doesn't make it so. All the same, I can believe it. If I do, reality, or my wife, will soon correct me.

Let me believe it, to see if it's true. Let me believe it, to see will it work for me. I truly believe that you, the reader, know what I mean. If I did not believe it, would it make any sense for me to proceed in this line of thinking? And if not a single reader who ever reads this knows what I mean, what have I lost? I have told what I truly believe and that in itself establishes me in myself as a human natural being.

Let me believe some more, to see what comes up.

What first comes up is my human nature. Now I may know it and see it.

*

If someone tells you that Elon Musk has developed a rocket that goes down instead of up, straight through the earth and out the other side, you believe it first. That's what you do as you try it on for size. You imagine it happening just inside that realm of belief. No use just trying to imagine it. Imagination doesn't work like that. First you have to believe. You don't know that you do it but there are a lot of things you do and you don't know that you do them. Believing is one of them. I call it real believing. It has probably been knocked out of you by your upbringing and education. Consequently, you say that you believe something when it fits in with your prejudices and your established principles (with what you like) and lastly also with your experiences – which themselves, of course, coincide with your prejudices, your fashionable discriminations and your modern narrow-mindedness.

So if I tell you about Elon Musk's rocket, you imagine it, you think about it and then you say: That's unbelievable! However you have already believed it in order to be able to figure out could it work. In reality it's not unbelievable, just unworkable – so far.

You might also wish to believe that by next March you will be able to fly to the Bahamas again, for your annual holiday. And what comes to light here is, that real believing can not be disappointed. If, by comparison, you just set your mind on it happening, that, indeed, might end in a disappointment, but if you truly believe it and when the time comes and no airplanes fly, then you continue to believe all the same, and you give up on that holiday ever so easily. Your believing is substantial. It does not depend on the vagaries of what goes on out there.

Now we can understand that believing is in fact a human natural attribute. When we truly believe, we are actually in touch and in contact with our human nature. When we're gullible, we've lost contact. When we are superstitious, we are energetically gullible.

*

The first time we make contact again with our human nature, after a period of 'in absentia', we are liable to get excited. This is something that happens. It's like falling in love. We want to shout out with glee: Hey ho! High ho! Then we look around. Did anyone hear that? Well, we didn't actually do it, we only 'felt like' shouting out. Still, that excitement is bubbling within us. Not inside us, but <u>within</u> us. Not the medical realm. There's a difference. It's not at all the same as when we're 'high' on sex or drugs or party-time. No, but we might, suddenly, decide to write a poem. We've never done it before but heck, here goes:

I'm not sure how to do this,
But here, if I don't, I'll regret.
As soon as I think I put down my drink
And lift up my spirit instead.

It doesn't make all that much sense at the moment but I feel I've gained something by doing it.

*

Our human nature seeks to contribute to our community. It hates to be prevented. This is important! We have prevented it long enough. It appears there's still a chance to make good what we've neglected. And oh dear, so much depends now on who we are and what we amount to. Our human nature, after all is not something else. It's incomparable. It's neither good nor bad, neither likeable nor disagreeable. It is what it is and there's nothing like it. No wonder we fought shy of it for so long, considering that the world we've lived in was a system and everything had to fit in before it was accepted. Our human nature, indeed, does not fit in. Not anywhere. It is the Outsider per se. Yours is not like mine and mine is not like Jeffrey Archer's. (I've forgotten who that is.)

So here I am faced with the existential problem per se. How am I going to present to my community that which is utterly different? Present it I shall, by hook or by crook, come hell or high water. The question is: How shall I make it – acceptable? No, that couldn't be right. I have, by now, forgotten entirely what those around me will accept and what they will reject. What to do? Am I to give up on my human nature because it will not 'fit in'? As soon as I entertain that notion even a little, my human nature becomes increasingly unacceptable. Interesting! So, instead of giving up on it, let me try the opposite. I shall love it. I shall love my human nature – this outsider.

Well, suddenly the sluice-gate opens. Happily I am able to love, that's all I can say. That which seemed impossible suddenly becomes more than possible. It is actual. How grateful I am now to those who showed me how to love and persuaded me to learn how to do it. I'm set. Little by little I shall learn how to make better and greater contributions to my community. Maturity has set in. I am about to turn into a mature human being. Watch this space.

*

My human nature is not what I mean when I say I. So is my nature separate from myself? It seems like an odd sort of a question. All the same, there are those who are relieved, commonly in the media, that they have finally learned how to love themselves. Do they perhaps mean that they have learned to love their human nature? That indeed they have discovered their human nature and that in the interest of its revelations they love it? One dearly hopes so. As for myself, I can love the one next to me as though he or she were I, but that is a far cry from loving that person like I love myself. I don't even like myself. When I love my neighbour, communal creativity is involved.

My guess is, that what people mean when they say they love themselves is not self-love but rather they finally feel they are no longer being judged by their social environment. It must be a relief. Enough said on that topic.

*

So what counts is that we discover our human nature and that we get ready for the revelations it wishes to make. From such as these, the kingdom of god on earth is constructed. Against that, it is quite possible and even rather fashionable these days, to assert oneself in the supernatural kingdom of god. Some who are members of certain Churches consider themselves to be in the kingdom of heaven or in the kingdom of god by dint of their church membership. What they mean, if they do really mean anything, is the kingdom of god as a supernatural entity. In other words, it does not involve their human nature. As a matter of fact, it operates as a substitute human nature. There is nothing creative about it. Once the kingdom of heaven is available to us in reality on earth, there is no longer any need for its supernatural entity, which does, after all, depend upon a popular corporeity.

So supernature is a substitute for human nature. I suppose you might say that we have a choice, to adopt one or to espouse the other. However it doesn't quite work like that. The two do not exist side by side, like tins of beans and tins of corn on a supermarket shelf. Only those who are endowed with revelation from their human nature can identify supernature and supernatural behaviour where it occurs. Those who exist supernaturally, live in their own reality and it is up to those who are aware of human nature and of its creative potential and reality to create a bridge to those who live supernaturally, because they alone understand the difference. While we are still establishing ourselves, this bridge is necessarily always a form of personal toleration.

Once our human nature is accessible to us and we have begun to create, we feel the need to hedge ourselves round while we identify what is going on with us. Unavoidably we will, for a time, resent any supernatural presence in our environment. We experience it as a sham. However, as a consequence, we do make greater efforts to establish ourselves as creative human beings.

Then comes the time when we feel secure in ourselves and we can, if we wish, reach out to those who live supernatural lives. We reach out in the same love by which we first greeted our own human nature. We reach out for the purpose of community, not at all critically in order to change anyone. If it so happens that someone is on the cusp of discovering his or her human nature, not only does nothing we do stand in his way but this lovely process of human community can begin.

Those who actually insist on their supernatural interpretation of reality and try to consolidate themselves in it by persuading others to adopt their brand or sect of it, are best avoided by those who live and love human-naturally and creatively.

A cult, even worse, is supernatural to the second power. People entrench themselves in a program of actual avoidance of human nature. These especially have to be avoided.

*

Due to the uniqueness of our human nature, and then to the complete authority of our human-natural creations, we stand alone, shoulder to shoulder with all others who are human natural. We cannot possibly be members of this or that religion, sect, club or party. We are whole and our task is to make whole and to bring to completion, creatively.

*

When we imagine the Christian West now, we may equally imagine the vast array of attempts to render a supernatural religion safe and secure against the inroads of pietism, realism and materialism and failing just precisely for the reason we mentioned above, namely the insistence of human nature on its innate rights and its unwillingness to be ignored.

What we cannot imagine is a successful religion once human nature reveals to us our personal contribution to the work of god's presence in the flesh, which is to say in all that is. Just as human nature creatively seeks to realize itself, so does merciful good spirit seek to participate in the resurrectional development and evolution of all beings on earth. It stands to reason that the renewal of all that lives and weaves on earth can only issue from the combined loving efforts of human beings and merciful, loving god. Such efforts are in no way supernatural but spiritual and human as one.

Since all that is, is human, it can be readily imagined how gradually all beings other than human beings will be drawn into this progress of renewal, from generation to generation and from moment to moment. That is how eternal life on earth is to continue endlessly, once all that is is new.

*

How supernatural man imagines the end of his supernatural state, if he imagines it at all rather than assuming that all will continue as is, this is bound to vary from one religion, creed or social system to the next. For the magnanimous historian, portraits are to be drawn and comparisons to can be made. What cannot be managed in any manner at all is a transition, imaginative or otherwise, from a supernaturally envisioned end-time to the time of renewal. This is illustrated by the fact that the meaning of apocalypse, a revelation of great knowledge, has been twisted to mean catastrophe and cataclysm. The great knowledge is nothing more and nothing less than human-natural revelation in the interest of renewal and eternal life on earth. So one supposes that what should really be made known is that any degree of breakdown is due to reaction to, and rejection of, knowledge. This is well enough known as common sense. The greater the new knowledge, the greater the initial reaction to it. Timely repentance and love of god during the search for eternal renewal reveals to each the contribution he can make to his community and all thoughts and images of Armageddon (the big hill) may be dismissed.

* *

Our creative acts are performed in the light of day. Whatever we do in the light of day is creative. This lets us know about the simultaneity of creation and the light of day. Here we have to keep in mind that the light of day is not the same as daylight. In fact how we see the light, and whether we see it at all, this is characteristic of our familiarity with human-natural creation. So this simple distinction we make between daylight and the light of day helps us to identify what we mean by nature. We know that the nature that is considered to be 'out there', the nature of the photographer and the modern scientist, for example, is not really believed. Therefore it is not real. It's acceptance is conditional on sensation-evidence and on theories extrapolated from that evidence. Basically, it is not real because not true.

It stands to reason that we see, or perceive, differently if we are human naturally creative and if reality is human-naturally revealed to us. If we are unaware of our human nature and ignorant of creation based on revealed knowledge, our perception will be biased in favour of knowledge from 'out there'. Our hunger for reality will be temporarily stilled by merely external evidence, which is to say by evidence based on mere appearances. Such appearances are not originally in contact with us but have to be pretended.

Nature will not reveal itself to us but it withdraws from us if we approach it as though it were a thing and an infinite number of things. No matter how insistently we refer to it as nature and both surround it and underpin with laws to keep it 'around', it withdraws all the same, or actually even more so, the more we try to fasten it down as unreal to the same measure as we are unreal.

This withdrawal of nature is, of course, not really noticed by the ignorant individual, who merely defines nature in accordance with how it appears to him to behave. He is never done documenting the ever increasing multiplicity of the things which he mistakes for natural beings.

Consider along with this that nature, as we have chosen to use this term in this essay, is in fact the face of the earth, its lively and colourful garment. The ignorant individual continues to document the texture of this garment and to analyse the face of this receding thing and what he ends up with is stuff which lend itself to his ingenious manipulation.

As the ignorant individual makes ever more complicated things from this stuff, the initially beautiful face of the earth turns ugly and the lively garment stiffens. The earth eventually is denuded and 'in a rage'.

Why were the natural endowments of the earth not appreciated? Why were live beings not enjoyed as they lived? Why was the beautiful face of the earth not loved?

Because human nature was not recognized for what it is, namely the source of revealed truths which allow human beings to overcome their ignorant individuality bent on extinct knowledge and merely apparent natural phenomena.

What we find if we let nature come to us rather than overpowering it with our arrogant will and our insistent intellect – given that we have learned the primary faith and a little wisdom to go with it – is a powerful stimulant to eternal life on earth. This go begin with. Then, gradually, nature, still the thing, reveals itself to our astonished eyes as nature, now the vast array of live beings, looking to us for solace and companionship. Lastly, as we continue to cooperate with merciful good spirit in terms of all the ends and goals of our revealed creations, nature becomes, in every imaginable sense, the mother of all beings, including human beings.

*

How we see has an effect on what we are looking at. Some people approach horses and the animals gladly perform for them. Some approach plants and they revive and gladly grow. As more and more of us learn how to see creatively, nature will revive. What we see when our seeing is connected to our human nature is not what we see when we seek its connection out there. Surely that makes sense. And sense has to be made. We do not make sense when we lose ourselves outside or inside. There's the photographic eye and there's the calculating eye. Neither of these is rooted in our humanity. Within us, in comparison now, our human nature longs for the light. It craves the light of day. That is an aspect of its definition. How unhappy it makes us if we refuse forever to accommodate it. Forget about the light with its theoretically constant speed. Put that as far back in your mind as possible. Consider, for a moment, the sunlight, that turns into daylight in reflection from everything you care to look at, the stars, the trees, your hand. Close your eyes now and remember what you looked at. Don't just recall it. Remember it. Dwell on it. Take the time for it. What we want is nature unlimited by our indwelling consciousness. Nature perhaps still fresh from god's garden. I am presently shining the light into which I was born on a natural example or two.

It means I have to overcome a few acquired prejudices and I'm more than glad to do that for you, the reader. There is nature within me, still in the dark, an there is nature without me, bright and shining. Each and every single creative act joins them up in personal fashion.

There is nature in here, dead as a doornail, trained and schooled into subsistence by the extinct sciences. Against that, god help me, there is nature within me, human nature, which allows me to refer to it and to treat it as mine, budding and burgeoning at present. What a discovery! Where have you been all my life, it cries, clasping my hands, thrilled to bits to meet me. You see, I explain, I had been told that I was not worthy. Quickly I write a poem. I praise the crops in the narrow fields, the deer that dare to develop their human contact anew. I rush about and learn the names of the wild flowers. I acquaint myself with the vast array of cloud design. I develop a weather eye. My inward nature laughs merrily and says: Don't overdo it. Respect the inborn measure of all that is wild and wonderful. If you come to grief, think of it as a momentary dysfunction calculated to increase your contact with your god-given body. No need to delve into the roots more than once. The roots take care of themselves. You'd be amazed if you knew what all goes on down there, all beneficial and thriving on multiple blessings. Now and again I may have to remind you of your humanity. Only imagine that you should be the one to forget, when every mosquito and termite and fungus and woodlouse whispers it day in, day out: Humanity! Humanity! Cool as a cucumber there, that mountain, shouts it out into the stratosphere. Humanity! All the biologies nibble at the invisible garment of the night, tasting humanity and hankering for a mouthful. Now you are on your way and I am with you. Let's keep it simple and straightforward. At least at the start. Once we have made a beginning, your eyes will see what has never existed for you until then. As we go on, every mere acquaintance turns, little by little, into feast and festivity, into praise and celebration.

*

Yes indeed – respect the inborn measure of all that is wild and wonderful. There's so much that needs to be said about that. As we come face to face – out here – with what is wild and wonderful, namely nature true and real, we are liable, momentarily, to fail to respect it.

So what is it we are liable to treat with indifference, keeping in mind that even this liability is inborn, in ourselves?

The inborn measure. In other words, not only is there no need for us to impose measure, nor could we get very far without making fools of ourselves if we tried.

Think only of what we might mean by that little word 'wild', we over-cultivated, over-civilized control-freaks. There are two ways to react in this case, as in all cases of successful renewal. We tighten up inside into a knot of anxiety because we have so thoroughly accustomed ourselves to dealing in inert concepts and dead processes. That's one way. Here is suddenly something that shakes off all shackles and manages to get right through to our soul. Help! We know all to well what the outcome of that is bound to be – CHAOS! In a hurry we check on all our customary comebacks to the threat of disorder and disarray – good grief! They do not apply. We panic.

That is one way. The other way could be described as liberty unchecked. We are flying high, in our supposed response to new nature wild and wonderful. We have finally arrived. Let's go 'whole hog'! We can handle it. We hear the voices of those who prophesy disaster and we shout those voices down with our own, super-liberated voice. "Cowards that you are! Look what we finally have! Nature unfettered and unbound!" We throw off our clothes and leap – into a thermal spring. That's us then, hard-boiled, insensitive for the rest of our life.

That's the other way. In both ways we behaved ignorantly; more to the point: unwisely. You might say that we did not behave. Behaviour in the face of ‘wild and wonderful nature’ is necessary. Lack of behaviour is drastic. Lack of behaviour ends in panic or in brutality.

And behaviour itself implies respect. Respect for the other. Respect true nature out here (not out there!) and find yourself in a privileged relationship with it. How is that? Why, your own human nature develops an affinity for it. Now you can handle the beauty of it, for one thing, and you can deal with the truth of it, for another. You have the skill for surviving and living in the presence of what is wild and wonderful, namely nature itself.

This could be put much more simply, but then it would have to bear the hallmarks of mystery, such as in a poem:

Roaring trade winds prowl from pole to pole,
A primrose blossoms by a thorny hedge,
Herds of reindeer move to greener pastures.
All that is human rises to the one occasion
While we remain behind, timid or unbridled.

Our passions drive us, now from fear to failure
And then we lack the courage for our dreams.
That human beings should wreck their humanity
Or neglect the very substance of their being,
This is the modern fashion of our tragedy.

We make a start by searching within ourselves
Until at last our nature is revealed to us
As human, not as timorous nor as arrogant.
Now we develop our essential being
And learn compassion, heart of human being.

New body, as new senses, is our gift.
Emotion, passion find their secret root.
To those who persevere, new world reveals
Largely empowered, its liberty and freedom
To us who learn behaviour and respect.

Incalculable nature draws us out
To teach us how to wonder at this wildness,
Which bears within itself its own constraint,
Relieving us of all responsibility
For taming, for explaining and for justifying.

What now remains for us is that we grow
Along with what reveals itself out here
Never as magic nor as supernature,
But as our preordained and royal home,
Its household our creative domesticity.

*

The inborn measure of all natural beings, of horses, of trees, of stones, of storms – if we can come to terms with this, we will no longer be tempted by mechanical manipulation, by the influence of the extinct sciences and arts. First, however, we have to be persuaded of our own inborn measure, and this is up to us, that we come to terms with it. Inborn measure – inward balance. Within us we have found it. We nourish and cherish it. Now we look beyond ourselves, so that we may lose ourselves in nature and its representatives. Just as we transplant our ego into the one we love, so do we now project it into all that is natural, including the one we love.

Is it then love that allows us to see a porcupine, a willow tree, as it is? 'As is' means 'in balance', possessed of inborn measure. Leaving a field of poppies alone, in the sense of not interfering with it, is not, after all, the same as respecting its inborn measure, as seeing myself as it, as being creative in terms of it. Let a farmer be creative in terms of his fields and his crops. Let him appreciate them for what they are in themselves, perfectly balanced in terms of world-existence. Like ourselves, to be sure. All other beings are like human beings, in their own way. We are able to appreciate that once we respect one another's authenticity prior to our own.

We cannot treat natural beings fairly, decently, while we still treat one another egotistically. First we persuade ourselves of the inarguable life-presence of one another, then this empowers us with the perception and insight to which fleas, flowers and flamingos existentially respond. Materialism, for but one thing, utterly denies any such perception and insight. The very imagination that builds bridges from us to all other natural beings is stultified by materialism. Nothing that is natural can thrive at the service of grasping self-interest. We turn into mere things and that is then how we see and abuse the live garment of the earth.

The Romance of nature is for poets to entertain us with. What is needed is the resurrection of nature, parallel to our own resurrection, as step by step we enter the kingdom of god on earth, leaving the modern world behind. All that is modern lacks measure, mutual respect and unconditional love. Nothing so much spurs us on to communal thinking, feeling and living as a correct perception of what modernism amounts to. When the modern world began, human beings stood face to face with the need to become truly human and each human being, through time, made his or her choice, for communal reality on earth or for a modern idealism that was self-devouring. Can we imagine now what it means for human beings if the modern age has come to its end? We are no longer being tempted like that. Can we continue in spite of the lack of this temptation? Even though it no longer tempts us, may the modernization process not continue apace, liberated from its duty to side-track the human being? Is the goal of modern man not to survive forever? Now he should be able to hand himself over gratefully to the machine, is that not correct? Behold the godly cyborg! Man as mere consciousness embedded in mechanical means.

What nonsense!

All the same, for human beings this might serve as the final entertainment. Imagine playing a glass-bead game with a mechanized humanoid! Like chess against a computer, only more intriguing.

*

You will be glad to know that Jean and Frank have come to an understanding. They have identified a few differences of opinion and struggled towards one or two agreements as to what might be worth talking about. We little realize sometimes how important it is to be able to talk. It seems we must have something to confess. Frank confessed he was no longer afraid of making a fool of himself and he offered numerous examples of his new-found courage, verbally, mostly. Jean's confession was of the sort that allowed her to exude feminine charm, and this threatened to constrict Frank in an increasing number of opportunities for making a fool of himself – I mean for demonstrating that he was no longer afraid of doing so. On the surface this would seem to place Jean in the ascendancy. However, not so.

"It's just that I need to put some of my convictions into practice," he said, hoping, thereby, to clarify his position.

She, decided to point out to him that not convictions but suppositions were more than likely what he was up against. The convictions might come later.

"Fine!" he stated, unperturbed. "My point is, that I have the genuine ambition to put life first, ahead of survival, don't you see." This, evidently, connected up with what they had been talking about before *we* came along. "This allotment, for example," he decided to illustrate, "could never rank quite as high in importance for me as my own development, my own growth as a human being. Even while I turn the soil over so that I can plant my shallots, I am dealing, inwardly, with that fatigue that comes over me during physical labour."

"Why do you labour, my dear?" she pointedly asked. The 'my dear' surprised me. They seem to have got on since last we met.

"Good point!" he agreed emphatically. "Why do I labour instead of working?"

"That's easy," she said. "You are wrapped up in yourself. – More orange juice, please! – You evidently get sucked into the very soil you turn over. It's as if you were digging your grave. I watched you. I felt sorry for you. The poor man, I thought. You'd think he was concerned for his survival."

"Thank you for the no doubt very useful critique," he announced. "Now what shall I do instead? How shall I behave instead? As soon as I take spade in hand I turn into a labourer. I have to finish the job as quickly and as efficiently as possible."

"Meanwhile you wreck yourself," she offered.

"Exactly! Oh, who will save me from my fate!"

"You said it yourself. Work instead of labouring." It seemed so plain and easy to her while she said it.

"Alright! Now we're getting somewhere. If labour is for survival, what is work for – if that doesn't sound too silly?"

"Let me see!" Evidently she had to think now. It was a ruse. She had made her mind up at least two minutes ago. "Work is for life," she said softly, casting a decidedly affectionate glance in his direction.

He smiled broadly. It was all so simple now. "Will I still be able to employ my manly muscles?" he inquired.

"Oh yes indeed!" she complied enthusiastically – and then corrected herself with: "Or rather no, not really, I fear. Muscles for life? No. It doesn't rhyme, does it. Muscles are of the flesh and the flesh is no use."

"Oh good heavens! How shall I turn the soil? Or must I cease from turning the soil?" He was only slightly perturbed, but he was perturbed.

"Let's for a moment look at it this way," she suggested. Next she looked this way and that way, as if gleaning information from the budding black currants and from the cumulus clouds up above. "Your interest for life as priority rather than for survival must originate in your human nature. Alright so far?"

He nodded.

“In other words not in feelings of scarcity of supply.”

“Oh, I see! Yes, I suppose so.”

“And what do we call the outward goal of our human nature?” She was wondering herself now and hoped he would come up with a legitimate response. He was taking his time, so she quickly added: “After all, your human nature wishes to show itself, does it not? Can we really believe that it is happy asleep in its cave like a hibernating bear?”

“No, we can not believe that,” he said. “Our human nature seeks to … join up with nature! That’s it! I’ve got it.”

“You do indeed.”

“Now, my dear Socrates,” he went on, “please tell us how it goes about that.”

“Why not tell me how <u>you</u> go about it,” she suggested.

“How about this,” he suggested. “When I work, I do not use my muscles but my wits.”

“Seems like a step in the right direction,” she thought. “It does leave open the possibility of mental labour, don't you feel?”

“So how about: When I work, rather than labouring, I submit myself to the beauty of nature. – Now do hold on, before you jump on that. I don't myself yet know what I mean. The beauty of nature? Nature without us, am I right? Not out there. Outwardly appreciated, eh? Something like that? Does that make sense?”

She hadn’t expected that. The beauty of nature? What was that, other than a beautiful sunset or the wind combing a field of wheat?

He noticed her consternation and added: “In response to the truth of our human nature, I was thinking. Is it silly? Do you think it’s silly, Jean?”

“No, not at all,” she said quietly. “It’s just that I have to think about it. What do you mean by it, in particular?

“Nature is glorious,” he reflected. I think that’s what I mean.

It might not be possible to talk about it. But I'm going to have it in mind next time I turn the earth over. It's bound to influence me."

"You, but not your muscles?" she suggested.

"Oh dear, this might be more than I can handle at the moment, Jean. I'm only a beginner when it comes to my human nature. I've only just begun to consider that as a possibility."

"What we might ask, even here and now," she suggested, sensitive to his reluctance to overreach himself, "is – how might we respond to the beauty of nature?'

"To the beauty that <u>is</u> nature?" he tentatively corrected. "I think of it as highly influential and effective. Like stepping into a field of life-stimulating impulses. It's what makes me feel so much better after entering these allotments and taking part in the business of food production."

"You suppose, you guess, that is what it's like, right, Frank? This is important. It's like that. But it's not that. Might it be impossible to say what it actually is? Might it be totally unimportant not being able to say what it actually is? Is the beauty that is nature perhaps like nothing else? So we have to believe it, and that's that?"

"And unless I believe it, my muscles take over?"

"It's astonishing, Frank, what we've discovered here, wouldn't you agree?"

"I would add that in future I shall approach nature with a degree of shyness."

"Well yes, that's a point, maybe. Just because we're walking among all these allotments, that doesn't mean we're in touch with nature, does it? I mean not really. We would have to decide, and to intend, to be in touch. I'm not even sure I could do it right now."

"Tell you what," he said, because a light had just come on in him, "how about we do it together. You and I, in unison. Shall we?"

"Of course," she agreed.

So they did. After a while they kissed. The most chaste kiss in creation.

After an appropriate silence he decided there was a bit more to say at the moment before he picked up spade again.

"I think of it now as a case of give and take, simultaneously – after that kiss," he said. When I take no account of nature, the beauty of it overwhelms me and tires me and fatigues me and that's part and parcel of my approach as a labourer. Now when I catch myself labouring, I will know it's high time to respond to the beauty that is nature."

"And you'll live, Frank!" she added, rather demonstratively.

"I'll have life while I work, and afterwards, rather than dying while I labour – while I labour ever so enthusiastically, ever so energetically – oh dear, that's a fact, isn't it? And I'll know I have more life after I've worked. Gosh, Jean, it's true, you're really quite beautiful, did you know that?"

She smiled sweetly and said: "Naturally!"

*

In good faith we may speak of outward reality and of inward reality. Inward reality concerns our humanity, our human being and our human nature. Our perfect, live approach to outward reality is symbolic. Of course we may choose to approach at any time what exists outside of us. If we do so with our mind and body as one, which is up to us, we happily come up not with outside, but with outward reality, which is finite and eternal, like ourselves.

Mind is thought, body is vision and feeling or passion. This is the case while our mind and body are one. The implication is that we may act symbolically. Symbolic action, now, is never thought alone or body alone, although thought may predominate or passion may preponder. So mere thought and vision or passion alone, individually, pertain to external or outside reality, which is not reality in good faith but in isolation and fragmented. The modern mind and the modern body are not capable of approaching outward reality. Their approach is not live, not perfect but imperfect, dissociative and thing- or data-oriented.

Anyone who wishes to succeed in doing anything good and useful for his environment will have to learn how to act symbolically. Only in that way can he overcome his modern habits of manipulating external reality, which disturbs the environment. Sadly these habits have long been couched in modernity and lately, in particular, in materialistic modernity. However there is no need to despair. Neither is there any benefit in analyzing materialism, in the hope of bending it in the direction of symbolic action. Symbolic action proceeds quite happily in good faith which is underpinned by selfless or unconditional love. Such love can be practiced and learned, and most successfully in our everyday behaviour and doing. Sadly academia has no use for it. Nor does the man or woman whose main concern is the financial profit margin.

To every symbolic action there is a reaction, and this reaction may again be utilized to further symbolic action. The reaction may be a simple rejection, so that someone simply says no, or it may be an attempt at utilization, where someone attempts to employ the symbolic content to further his own ends. The one who has acted symbolically is only momentarily and superficially swayed by such reactions before he embodies, or envisions, or impassions them. This sounds complicated, but it merely describes what the one who has acted symbolically will notice himself doing while he replies to such reactions with love.

*

A symbolic act interferes with our present environment and always in line with improvement and investment. We may see what we intend to act upon as dual, such when we see two sides to a question or when theory and practice refuse to match. This however is not to cause us to refrain from action, for upon patient contemplation our symbolic approach will allow us to arrive at a perfect solution to the problem.

Even our intention has to be symbolic, not either realistic or idealistic. We do well to keep in mind right from the start that the very urge within us to act is the same as the apparent need of the environment to be acted upon. As human beings we do not stand aloof or aside from outward reality. To put it poetically, what goes on out here dovetails with what goes on in here. It may have taken us years to arrive at this insight. Some, these days, are born with it. Imagination plays the role of a linchpin in that it is always happy to show us how the two are one, though never statically one. In other words, we cannot picture it.

The symbolic intention makes no difference between being out here and being in here, between outward and inward being. Of course there is always the temptation to veer off to one side or the other, to consider this side or the other side, and this temptation needs to be recognized and simply ignored. It would be wrong to engage with it. After all each one of us approaches environment from his or her own view and any attempt to speak of the environment as such is not useful once we wish to get down to making a useful contribution. As soon as we feel there is something for us to do, we take responsibility for the way we ourselves see it, without getting side-tracked by myths, ideals or abstractions.

Private or public endeavours, by individuals or governments, can certainly draw attention to where and how the environment is ailing. Private of public action, however, will merely shift problems from one area of experience to another, creating illusion of progress. Surprisingly, it is just such illusion that prompts individual human beings to come up with symbolic action – which fundamentally aligns outward shortfall with inward surfeit, or vice versa.

The goal to be achieved, time after time, occasion after occasion, is existential balance. We might put it like this: as human beings grow, their environment grows with them and as our environment changes we tend to join in – which draws attention to our overall communal responsibility for health of environment along with human wellbeing.

So when we imagine nature alongside human nature, we equally imagine human beings alongside their environment. It amounts to the same symbolic relationship. It is in fact our distinct imagination that allows us to do this in the interest of creatively beneficial exchange. No one can stand back from the environment and make useful pronouncements because this implies his or her static point of view, which can only ever be illusively helpful. Another way of putting it would be: While we are not embedded in our environment and aware of our longing to evolve, our comments on the environment will at best be superficial and at worst misleading.

Our natural environment, whether or not we appreciate it fairly and clearly, always and eternally changes, meaning that it changes whether we are aware of it or not. Once we are beautifully at peace with our environment it does not occur to us to consider that it changes, because we change right along with it. When we have stepped into the stream and raised our feet off the ground, we no longer think about the stream but we enjoy the passing pageant of the shore on both sides. Until that time, however, we speak of change so as to remind ourselves of our deadly tendency to become static and lifeless while we still, perhaps, recall a time when we were persuaded to involve ourselves in the materialistic philosophies and points of view that strove to shut out any consideration of mutual change. Happily those days are behind us. We are at liberty to contemplate symbiotic relationships and free to act symbolically if we wish to contribute to an ever more healthy environment.

*

So what about Frank and Jean now, what are they up to and

have they come to a more permanent arrangement – with each other, I mean?

Of course they have. You might say they have joined up their separate allotments. They have come to the conclusion that each, separately, can lead a life of sorts and if not too many mistakes are made and if there is enough social involvement to go around while 'the health' holds out and so on, the singular existence might be supportable. That was all they had in mind until they met: she a liberated woman, he a man with his work plus a hobby. It would have been a loveless existence, even if they had learned to care for their fellow man and managed to get involved in social work, which gains us a satisfaction of sorts.

Instead they fell in love and right away loved each other. Happily, when they fell, they were mature enough to realize that after falling we do well to rise again, as soon as possible. Gradually, I am happy to say, they are discovering each other's faults and realizing that they are their own, if you can make sense of that. The Covid epidemic had not started yet, however they did not need it to be reminded that in order to become one, each of the two has to remain far enough apart from the other to be able to sustain a clear view of 'my' business and 'his' or 'her' business. In other words they eschewed sex and started a family. Now they have two children and another on the way.

I mention it to remind of the beautiful truth that, both within and without us, nature and human nature, while rooted in one and the same person, may be approached integrally, in distinction, and then we enjoy life as it is meant to be lived.

* * *

www.ingramcontent.com/pod-product-compliance
Ingram Content Group UK Ltd.
Pitfield, Milton Keynes, MK11 3LW, UK
UKHW020418250726
13967UKWH00007B/2705